SOUTHERN REGION THROUGH THE 1950S

Year By Year

MICHAEL HYMANS

AMBERLEY

First published 2017

Amberley Publishing
The Hill, Stroud
Gloucestershire, GL5 4EP

www.amberley-books.com

British Library Cataloguing in Publication Data.
A catalogue record for this book is available from the British Library.

ISBN 978 1 4456 6619 8 (print)
ISBN 978 1 4456 6620 4 (ebook)

Typeset in 10.5pt on 13pt Sabon.
Origination by Amberley Publishing.
Printed in the UK.

Contents

Preface

The Southern Railway ceased to be on 1 January 1948, when the railways were nationalised and it became the Southern Region of British Railways. Being born and raised in Sussex during the 1950s and 1960s, to me it was always just 'The Southern', hence the title of this book.

Nationalisation had not only brought the railways into public ownership but road freight and passenger transport as well. As the decade progressed, these reverted to private ownership, which had serious repercussions for the railways.

The book relates how 'The Southern' evolved through the 1950s. It contains a diary of events, major and trivial, but all interesting. It does not claim to be a definitive history of the railway but attempts to demonstrate how the region recovered after being left in a very run-down state after the Second World War.

The Modernisation Plan of 1955 paved the way for massive investment in the railways, which financed the expansion of the third rail electrical system in Kent and the start of the rundown of steam in favour of diesels throughout the region.

While researching the book, it amazed me how quickly the service was up and running again after accidents, with one driver just carrying on after a fatal collision with a lorry on an occupational crossing. Compare this with the time it took to restore the service on the Croydon Tramway after the accident in 2016.

Many of the figures quoted in the book are for the railways as a whole, as figures that relate solely to the Southern are not available.

I have consulted numerous articles from various railway magazines of the period as well as some superb websites, so I am indebted to many unknown contributors. The majority of images are from a private collection I acquired and have not been published before.

Chapter 1

1950

Brighton Line Resignalling

In 1946, the Southern Railway had decided to complete the resignalling of the Brighton line using multi-aspect colour light signals instead of the semaphore signals being used at the time. This would entail altering the signals from Coulsdon North to Battersea Park on the Victoria line, and to Bricklayers Arms Junction on the line to London Bridge. Signalling into the termini had already been converted to colour light from these points. The cost of these improvements was £1.75 million. The line south of Coulsdon North had already been converted in the mid-1930s, but further work was interrupted by the war. The scheme was split into four sections and it was envisaged it would be completed in 1955.

In 1950 the first stage of quadruple track from Bricklayers Arms Junction to Norwood Junction North was completed and brought into use on 8 October. Three new signal boxes were built at Bricklayers Arms Junction (fifty-five levers), New Cross Gate (seventy-one levers) and Forest Hill (forty-seven levers). These replaced eight boxes that contained 279 levers. The thirty-eight new signals allowed a headway of two-and-a-half minutes between stopping trains. The new boxes incorporated maintenance staff accommodation, relay apparatus rooms and accumulator rooms. Telephones were provided at every signal to give train crews direct access to the signalmen. Points within 500 yards of the signal boxes were operated directly, whereas those further afield were operated using relays.

New Terminal for Southampton

Foreign holidays and cruises were becoming popular and at Southampton Docks a new passenger and cargo terminal was opened by Clement Attlee – the Prime Minister – on 31 July. It had been planned during Southern days and measured over 1,000 feet long; it was able to accommodate two full-length boat trains. The operation and management of the dock passed from the Railway Executive to the Docks and Inland Waterways Executive on 1 September.

New Locomotive Cab Design put on Show

A full-size mock-up cab was constructed to show the positioning of controls that would be used on all the new standard locomotives to be constructed. It was on view at the Executive's headquarters and locomotive crews were invited to come along and give their opinion on the new layout. This was part of an initiative to improve relations between management and staff. The cab was based on 70000 *Britannia* and included the tender and rear part of the boiler, so that visibility from the cab could be assessed.

Improvements for the crews included: much better weather protection; controls being conveniently grouped on either side for driver or fireman; lockers for their food; the placement of the majority of steam pipes outside the cab to keep down temperatures; setting the large front windows – which could be opened for easy cleaning – at an angle to eliminate glare; incorporating a sliding cab roof and side windows to aid ventilation.

Repairs to Bopeep

Bopeep Tunnel between and St Leonards Warrior Square and West St Leonards, where the routes to London and Eastbourne diverge, had to be closed for repairs. Apart from regular maintenance, the tunnel had not caused any major problems during its 100-year life, even though considerable amounts of water found its way into the tunnel and had to be taken away by a centre drain.

However, in September 1949, large cracks were found in the side walls around 150 yards from the western end, as well as inward movements of the walls leading to upward movement of the track. A series of reinforced concrete inverts were installed, which meant the track had to be singled throughout its length. Further examinations revealed more deterioration and it was decided to close the tunnel completely, giving the Chief Civil Engineer complete possession from 27 November. All services to Hastings from London via Tunbridge Wells were diverted to Bexhill West and the coastal services were terminated at St Leonards (West Marina), with those wishing to continue to Hastings having to resort to replacement bus services. Electric lights were installed in the tunnel to aid visibility and it was concluded that after an exceptionally dry summer, the percolation of water had gradually weakened the ground behind the brickwork.

The closure of the tunnel not only caused problems for passengers, but for the operating department as well. The only way Hastings Station could be reached by rail was via the line from Ashford, and that had a number of weak bridges. Before the closure of Bopeep Tunnel, the Schools class had been forbidden to use the Ashford line, but this restriction was lifted subject to a speed limit of 40 mph being imposed. This led to the situation of locos reaching Hastings Station and being within 2 miles of their home shed, but ultimately unable to reach there without a diversion via Ashford, London and Battle – a journey that sometimes took days. The tunnel reopened on 5 June 1950.

Accidents

On 1 February, an inter-regional train from Ramsgate to Birkenhead collided with a car on the level crossing at East Shalford, on the line from Reigate to Guildford. Two men in the Morris saloon were killed instantly. The subsequent report into the accident found that the young female crossing keeper had phoned the signalman to ascertain that it was safe to open the gates, and had been told not to open them until the Down train had passed. Unfortunately, an Up train passed and the crossing keeper – who admitted to becoming confused as to Up and Down lines – opened the gates, allowing the car to start to cross. Neither the crew nor the signalman were blamed, although it was said that the latter – who had only been passed out twenty-five minutes before the accident (his examiner was still in the box with him) – could have mentioned that a train was approaching from both directions.

Another accident occurred on a crossing on 24 April. This one occurred on an occupational crossing at Boarers Manor Way between Belvedere and Abbey Wood. An area of private land had been used for a while by Romani travellers and the crossing had been a cause for concern for a while among train drivers due to several incidents at the site caused by the crossing gates being left open and horses wandering on to the track. On this day, visibility was bad because of rain, and a lorry with three adults and a baby started to cross into the path of two approaching electric trains. One managed to stop, but the other did not. The driver said he noticed the lorry starting to cross when he was only around 50 yards away. He released the 'dead man's handle' and took cover. He stopped with seven coaches over the crossing, but the last one still straddling it. He was unhurt, climbed down from his cab and walked back to the crossing. The baby was unfortunately killed. After making sure that the injured were being cared for and that there was no significant damage to his train, he climbed back into his cab and proceeded to London Bridge. How times have changed!

New Stock and Withdrawals

A shortage of stock was still an issue, but nationwide a further eighty-seven new locomotives, 376 passenger carriages and over 6,000 wagons of various types were introduced in the first three months of the year.

The light Pacifics were still being built and Eastleigh had just been assigned an order to build six more (34095/7/9/101/2/4). It had also been thought that the last West Country – No. 34110 66 *Squadron* – was to be built with two outside cylinders and Walschaerts valve gear, but constructional difficulties had caused this to be abandoned.

10201 was the first mainline diesel to be introduced on the Southern when it made its debut in November 1950. It had been designed by O. V. S. Bulleid as long ago as 1946, but financial reservations had held up its manufacture. Even then, Southern spotters had to wait a while to see it as it was sent for trials on the LMS between St Pancras and Derby, and then it was on show at the Festival of Britain Exhibition. Numbers 10201 and 10202 were eventually put to work on trains from

Waterloo to Weymouth and Exeter. The locos were powered by 1,500 hp diesel electric engines with six axle-hung traction motors attached to the three driving axles on either bogie. The bodies were contoured to match that of Bulleid's coaches. The cabs were not only fitted with the controls needed to drive the engine, but also an electric cooker, hand-wash basin, and a lavatory. Heating was supplied to carriages by an oil-fired boiler. When hauling eleven bogie coaches from Weymouth, they often needed to be piloted as far as Bournemouth. This was often done by a U class 2-6-0. Previously, these loads were banked as far as Bincombe Tunnel, as it was not allowed for a steam locomotive to pilot a diesel, but the rules were changed to allow piloting.

Two double-deck electric four-car trains entered service around the start of 1950. They had been built at Lancing to a design by Bulleid in an effort to try to ease the overcrowding between Dartford and Charing Cross. Adding more carriages to trains to solve the problem was not an option due to the lengths of platforms. Each unit could seat 508 compared to 386 on a 4-SUB. They were classified as 4DD and numbered 4001/2. They were not popular with crews or passengers and no more were built, but these two survived until October 1971 when they were withdrawn. The carriages survive and 4002 is being restored.

Loco Movements

The war had seen many locomotives having their working lives extended, and an article in a 1950 *Railway Magazine* by an enthusiast recorded many of the engines he had recently seen.

At Horsham he had witnessed a D1 0-4-2T designed by William Stroudley still in Southern green – albeit somewhat faded – that was nearing the end of its life. More common were Robert Billinton's D3 and Dugold Drummond's M7 0-4-4Ts on passenger services north to Guildford and south to Brighton. E3, E4 and E5 0-6-2 radial tanks were also common sights on un-electrified branch lines. New LMR type 2-6-4 tanks built at Brighton could also be seen on running in duties.

One Saturday in 1950, an intrepid traveller boarded a Birmingham-bound train that left Hastings at 10:45 a.m. and made himself comfortable in the dining car of the ten-coach maroon train. The first leg of the journey was to Eastbourne and this was pulled by a Marsh I3 4-6-2 tank 32077.

On arrival at Eastbourne there was a change of power to an LMR type 2-6-4T 42096. While waiting at Eastbourne, he noticed another inter-regional train; this one was bound for Leicester with 32325 – a Marsh 4-4-2 tank built in 1910 – at the front. This train had also started at Hastings and had arrived in Eastbourne behind a Q1 0-6-0.

Continuing his journey, another change of loco was needed when reversing at Brighton. Many more passengers boarded here and, although a West Country was booked for the duty, a 2-6-0 U1 coupled up. Despite the difference in power, 60 mph was maintained for much of the journey, with a top speed of 65 mph being attained. A Black 5 was waiting at Willesden to take the train on further. The Leicester-bound train seen at Eastbourne also went via Willesden arriving behind Class H2 4-4-2 32424 *Beachy Head*. It handed its train over to an LMS Coronation class in blue livery.

Redhill was another station where engines were changed on inter-regional services. Trains coming from Kent and the Sussex coast split or joined there and WR 2-6-0s took or brought the trains to and from Reading and further afield.

Excursion traffic was always popular with young trainspotters as maroon coaches from the LMR, and chocolate/cream from the WR, made a change from the sea of green Southern stock.

The summer timetable for 1950 shows a daily service from Birkenhead to Margate. Inhabitants of Birmingham were spoilt with a list of Sussex destinations of Brighton, Eastbourne and Hastings. Mancunians also enjoyed a through service to Sussex resorts. There was also a Saturday's-only service from Nottingham to Ramsgate and from Birmingham to Margate. From Bournemouth there were services to and from Sheffield and Oxford.

Bulleid's Leader

In May it was reported the Bulleid's leader 36001 had not moved from Brighton shed for several days, while 36002/4 were still in the works, and 36003 had been in the electric car shed for some time.

At the end of June, 36001 was undergoing nocturnal tests between Eastleigh and Woking with a ten-coach train. Previously, it had been seen working a similar train between Eastleigh and Fratton. It seemed to be working well but rumours were circulating about steaming difficulties due to the reduced size of the firebox, caused by the increased size of the firebox walls. Problems occurred later in the year when, in August, the chain operating the mechanical lubricator broke at Guildford. Later the same month, when operating with an increased load, it 'sat down' on Micheldever Bank due to a shortage of steam. It returned to Brighton Works where it was fitted with a new set of piston rings.

Another of Bulleid's designs had just entered service. This was the diesel mechanical shunter 11001. It was based at Norwood Junction and not only used as a yard and hump shunter, but also on inter-regional freights. Its 500 hp, twelve-cylinder Paxman engine gave it a top speed of 36 mph. It had dual controls that meant it could be driven from either side, and incorporated the usual foot-operated dead man's handle.

Some Facts and Figures

These figures relate to the network as a whole as results for the Southern Region only are not available, but give an indication as to how the railways fared throughout the decade. Gross receipts were £340 million and, with expenditure of £314 million, this left an operating profit of £26 million. Over 73 million parcels were shipped by passenger trains. Container traffic was increasing and 23,000 containers were now on the network, compared with 15,000 in 1938. Collection and delivery services were handled by 4,700 horses, 8,200 mechanical horses, and 5,600 rigid lorries. Overall, 281 million tons of freight were moved. There were 19,598 steam, 10 electric, and 148 diesel/gas turbine locomotives worth £104 million. Life-expectancy of locomotives had to be increased to forty years from thirty-three before the war. Replacing the entire fleet would cost £200 million.

Operating these took 92,255 drivers, motormen, firemen and cleaners, backed up by 15,889 shed staff, with another 54,369 in workshops. Working expenses included £88 million for fuel and wages, and £23 million was spent on maintenance. Depreciation of assets was £2.4 million.

The locos were responsible for pulling 42,000 coaches and 1.1 million wagons. 122 ships were also owned.

Miscellanea

In Kent, it was reported that many of Stirling's engines had been withdrawn and that those that had survived were relegated to branch line work. D1s and E1s could still be seen, especially on busy summer Saturdays and on hop pickers specials. A few Ls and L1s could still be seen in malachite-green and, in contrast, the new class of Merchant Navys (MN) in experimental blue livery had been noted.

Horley, just north of Gatwick, was being used to scrap condemned locomotives. It was not the first time the site had been used for this purpose, as a siding was used by the LBSCR for the same purpose. The first locos to go under the cutter's torch in the new era were Drummond 4-4-0s 171 and 345 and Adams 4-4-0 657.

Further west, the practice of changing all engines at Salisbury and Exeter Central had been discontinued in February. This resulted in a daily saving of fourteen engines and nineteen footplate crews.

A typical turn for a Nine Elms locomotive was Nine Elms Duty 5 (Merchant Navy):

10.50 a. m.	Nine Elms to Exeter Central	(passenger)
6.48 p.m.	Exeter Central to Templecombe	(perishable)
9.50 p.m.	Templecombe to Clapham Junction	(milk)

Some Battle of Britain class locos had been struggling when assigned to the Night Ferry from Dover and had needed assistance, so Merchant Navys 35028/9/30 were assigned to the Eastern section to take over these duties.

On 6 July, a Special conveying Her Majesty from Victoria to Cranbrook was hauled by E1 class 4-4-0 31067.

Electric locomotive 20003 was repainted in black livery with aluminium coloured bogies, roof, and numerals, which means that all three electric locos were in different liveries, with 20002 in blue, and 20001 in malachite-green.

Apart from running the railways, the British Transport Commission (BTC) also ran the shipping services from the country's ports, of which the Southern had a large share. Figures are not available for the financial results of individual ports, but the shipping operation as a whole made a profit of £2.85 million.

The famous speeded-up cine film *London to Brighton in Four Minutes*, filmed from the cab of an electric unit, was released and, unbelievably, some people phoned Waterloo to ask when the new service was to start!

Cheap off-peak fares were becoming very popular, with ticket sales in 1948 showing a 100 per cent increase on the previous year. These were introduced to give the public the chance to enjoy a day out. Five-, six-, or seven-day tickets had also been made available, allowing short breaks and holidays to become affordable.

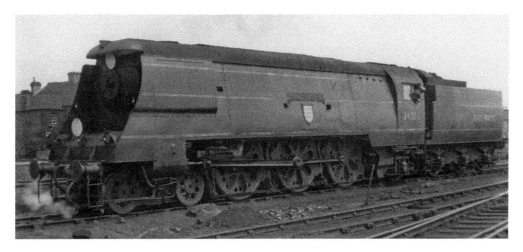

West Country 34002 *Salisbury* was still in malachite green livery, but had lost its Southern identity and original 21C102 number in favour of British Railways markings on the tender when photographed on 6 August 1949. The headcode indicates that it may have been on a Waterloo to Plymouth service.

Another engine still bearing its Southern identity was N15 King Arthur 449 *Sir Torre* on 9 July 1949. It was photographed at Eastleigh, attached to a Drummond eight-wheeled watercart from a G14. It was introduced in June 1925 and withdrawn in December 1959.

Bulleid's new diesel shunter 11001 at Norwood Junction. Note it carried steam style headcodes.

Class T14 443 was photographed at Eastleigh with an eight-wheel watercart. The class were rebuilt in 1931 from Drummond engines introduced in 1911. They suffered from high coal and water consumption and hot axle boxes. 443 was nearing the end of its life here and all the class had been withdrawn by June 1951.

1271 was a C class goods engine designed by Wainwright for the SECR. There were 109 in the class that were introduced between 1900 and 1908. All but two survived into BR ownership.

Another C2X, this time is 32546 in BR livery with lion on wheel decal. Filmed on the same day as the previous image and at Norwood Junction, their home shed.

Some C2Xs had twin domes and 32532 was one of those. Filmed on 10 June 1950 before the 'BRITISH RAILWAYS' on the tender was changed for the lion on wheel logo. It had been built as a C2 in October 1900 and was converted to a C2X with a larger boiler in July 1911, which it kept for nearly fifty years before being withdrawn in May 1960.

Norwood Junction shed was again the site for this portrait of C2X 32554. It had received its BR number, but not any crests, on 21 October 1950.

The N15s were known as King Arthurs, owing to the names given to them. *The Red Knight*, photographed at Eastleigh, was still in SR livery before its number 755 became 30755. The headcode suggests that it could be readied to take over a Plymouth to Waterloo service.

A good side shot of 30850 *Lord Nelson*, newly adorned with BR's express passenger lined green livery. It was attached to an eight-wheel bogie tender. This was the prototype of sixteen examples. It was built in 1926, two years before the rest of the class entered service.

On 5 August 1950 C1 still bore its original number. This was Bulleid's numbering system where the 'C' stood for three coupled axles and the '1' for the first in its class. It was soon to become 33001.

30792 *Sir Hervis de Revel* was an N15 King Arthur class built in 1925. It succumbed to the cutter's torch in February 1959.

1390 started life a Class O 0-6-0, designed by James Stirling in 1878. It was his first design after joining the SER from the GSWR in Scotland. In December 1915 it was reboilered and designated Class O1. It was near the end of its life here, as it was withdrawn in April 1951.

W3 *Ryde*, an E1 0-6-0T, was photographed at Newport.

Chapter 2

1951

Report into Future Motive Power

1951 saw the publication of the Railway Executive's 181-page report into 'Motive Power'. A committee had been set up by the Executive to produce an extensive report that was to have far-reaching effects over the next twenty years, so it is worth looking at in some detail.

Nationalisation had provided the opportunity to consider the nation's requirements as a whole. The Executive concluded that, as British manufacturers had successfully produced both diesel and electric locomotives for foreign purchasers, they could produce either form of traction to meet the requirements of British Railways. The Executive also concluded that gas turbine and atomic energy were still at too much of an experimental stage to be considered.

Locomotives were expected to have a working life of thirty to fifty years, so they foresaw that any change to a different form of motive power would have to be a long-term strategy to avoid a waste of capital expenditure. This would be advantageous in that the slow change would be within the capabilities of British industry at the time, but also disadvantageous in that any advances in technology would take a long time to be applied to the fleet. The recent war was still fresh in people's memories, and relying on imported oil for fuel over the plentiful supply of home-grown coal could have played a great part in decisions made for the future. The Executive decided, however, that without any advice from the Minister of Transport, any decision would be made on purely financial grounds.

The Executive looked at the American system, where there had been a rapid changeover to diesels from steam, but commented that, in the States, there were not so many restrictions on capital spending due to the war. They also noted that the operating companies did not build their own locomotives, but normally hired them from separate train-building companies instead. These train companies limited the types they built and benefited from economies of scale, with their diesels only costing three times as much to build as a steam engine, compared to four times as much in the UK.

Looking into the future, increased competition from roads was envisaged, but it was also thought that thirty to forty-seat helicopters would be developed, and that these would form a kind of Inter City service along the lines of 'Green Line' coaches.

The report went on to state that they envisaged lighter and faster express trains maintaining speeds of 80 mph, but also thought that weekend-excursion trains would still be heavily laden, and the demand for these would increase, especially if cheap fares were offered. On the downside, it was thought that many branch lines and intermediate stations could be closed, with buses being able to give a better service.

When it came to freight services, it was also envisaged that customers would want a 'next-day' delivery service. This would entail having generally shorter freight trains able to maintain higher speeds, capable of keeping up with overnight sleeper or parcels services. One of the problems faced with speeding-up freight trains was that many older wagons were still fitted with grease-lubricated axle boxes, which tended to overheat when running at anything other than slow speeds. Other problems included the fact that the majority of the old wagons were still fitted with loose three link couplings, as well as their lack of continuous brakes. At that time, there was no plan to replace these wagons.

The way the public viewed their railways also had to be taken into account. Badly maintained locomotives having to use poor-quality coal had added to the amount of black smoke being emitted from engines, which not only settled on station buildings and furniture, but also found its way through open carriage windows to settle on seats and passengers' clothes. This dirt had a bearing on the design and colour that could be used for seating materials; the brighter colours becoming more popular with the public could not be used as they quickly became soiled and discoloured. Keeping the infrastructure clean and presentable to the public was an additional cost, compared to diesel or electric systems.

The use of better coal would help with the problem, but would not alleviate it altogether. The relatively small dimensions of fireboxes on British locomotives compared to foreign engines dictated that 'large coal' needed to be used for maximum efficiency. It was important to the committee to ascertain whether supplies of affordable large coal would be guaranteed in the future. The cost of large coal had almost tripled since 1938 to 49s 7d per ton. This was the price at the pithead and did not take into account the large costs of distributing the coal to engine sheds. Only 30 per cent of coal produced was large coal, and this percentage had been steadily declining. The railways used 13.75 million tons in 1950 and were in competition with other users. Exports for this coal meant the Coal Board could not guarantee meeting the railway's demands in the future.

Electrification was then considered and in 1931 the Weir Report stated that in order to run a comparable service, only 3.6 million tons of lower-grade coal would be needed to power the network, compared with the 13.4 million tons steam engines were using at the time. Savings would be achieved by locomotives on standby duties not using any fuel. Electric trains in service would also not be drawing current when coasting or braking. The British Electrical Authority assured the committee that they could meet the increased demand needed by the railways, as they foresaw that some dieselisation would mean not all lines would be electrified, and that any changeover would be gradual – allowing them time to build any additional power stations needed.

One concern was that an electrified railway would be more vulnerable to air attack, but having a national grid would ensure that, should a power station be attacked, supplies could be obtained from a different source. It had been found on the Continent that in localised attacks, the overhead lines took no longer to fix than the track beneath them, so the lines were not closed for any longer.

When dieselisation was considered, the main concern was continuity of supply, as all fuel would need to be imported and paid for in foreign currency. However, world production of crude oil had doubled since 1938 to 540 million tons. The oil industry had plans to refine the crude oil imported into this country and envisaged that, by 1954, 25 million tons would be refined every year – an increase of around 100 per cent on the 1950 figure.

Complete dieselisation would need an annual usage of 3 million tons, but the oil industry assured the committee that these demands could be met – especially as oil production was increasing annually. They were, however, aware that there had been problems in paying for imported oil and that the political situation in Persia and the Middle East could not be ignored.

It was noted that, in Britain, the railways were virtually alone in building their own locomotives – other countries purchased them from private manufacturers. Changing to this method would obviously have a massive effect on railway workshops, but it was put forward that diesel engines or electric traction motors could be bought from an outside source and fitted to chassis and bodies designed and built in Railway Executive workshops. Although there were few operating at home, there were many British-built electric and diesel engines operating successfully in different parts of the world, and their order books were full. The committee were advised that there would not be a need to build new workshops to construct newer forms of traction, but existing facilities could be converted successfully, depending on the goodwill and co-operation of existing staff.

The role and lives of the footplate staff were also considered. It was becoming increasingly difficult to recruit and maintain the staff needed to operate steam services – not just the footplate crews, but those at sheds who had to dispose of the ash and keep the engines in presentable condition. The arduous nature of driving and firing a steam loco led to relatively high sickness levels, which meant that a high number of staff was needed to be on duty to cover sickness. In Switzerland, it had been noted that sickness levels had dropped considerably since they had electrified their system.

Dieselisation or electrification would mean that depots would be cleaner, more attractive places to work, with the nature of work becoming more specialised than menial as washing plants replaced cleaners. Changing over to newer forms of traction would also mean that those wishing to become drivers would not have to start off as cleaners, which, with newer, cleaner job opportunities being created in other walks of life, was putting many off.

It was also noted that either form of traction would do away with the need to change engines on very long journeys. Steam locomotives, on reaching the end of their journeys, often had to go to a shed to have their coal and water supplies replenished before making another trip. This not only took up time but often entailed running over lines needed for other services, taking time or causing possible disruption. Availability of locomotives was also increased, with either system meaning that fewer engines would need to be built and maintained. Savings could also be made in quicker turn round times at termini, better acceleration, and increased speeds up inclines – but the main point of saving would be due to only needing one man in the cab. It was acknowledged that two men were used in all diesels and electric locomotives at that time, but it was pointed out that many European countries manned their trains with only one. However, in this country, the railway unions were against any reduction of footplate manning levels. The committee felt that the difference in running costs between one and two men could have a large bearing on the decision of what motive power would be chosen in the future.

Initial costs of building steam engines were much less than diesel or electric locos. The cost of building a new Britannia Class 4-6-2 was £22,600, whereas a Brighton-built 2-6-4T was £14,400. The cheapest of the new BR Standard engines was the Class 2 2-6-2T, which cost only £6,200.

Bearing in mind the advantages and disadvantages of steam, the committee came to the conclusion that, as there were still 19,500 steam locos in service, it would take some time to replace these entirely, so pursuing improvements in running costs by using better coal and improving firing techniques, for example, were still seen as viable options.

The committee then turned its mind to electrification and noted that at the start of 1951, 925 route miles out of a total of 19,471 had already been electrified. These were mainly suburban services from major cities, where turn round times at major termini had to be kept to a minimum. Much of this was on the Southern.

An Inter-Executive Committee report of 1950 recommended that future electrification should be on the 1,500 DC system except for the Southern, which should keep to its present 750 DC third rail system. Advantages of electric traction over steam were stated as greater availability of locomotives, size of power unit, quicker turn round times at termini, better acceleration and uphill speeds, freedom from smoke, stimulation of traffic, and better working conditions for staff. One disadvantage was the possibility of widespread disruption should the power supply be cut for any reason, wherein every locomotive within an area would be rendered unusable. The Weir Commission – which had been set up in 1931 to look into electrification – estimated that to convert every line in the country to electric traction would cost £341 million; at least £1 billion in 1951. On the Southern in particular, it was noted that some steam services were running over routes that were partially electrified – for example, a steam train from London to Ramsgate (76 miles) ran as far as Gillingham (36 miles electrified), and from London to Dover (78 miles) and Folkestone (72 miles), the first 23 miles (to Sevenoaks) were electrified.

Both routes lent themselves to multiple-unit working over their entire distance. To finish electrifying the Central and Eastern sections would mean converting another 623 route miles beyond the 714 already electrified. Before nationalisation, the Southern had put forward a revised scheme that would entail electrifying a further 284 route miles, but leaving other secondary routes to be run by diesel traction.

Diesel traction was then looked at, but the Committee had little experience of diesel power on BR to draw conclusions from. The LMSR had two locos 10000/1 built in 1947, and the Southern also had two – Bulleid's 1Co-Co1 10201/2, which had only just been introduced – with a third on order. Even with little data to go on, and teething troubles that led to more maintenance than would be expected with a larger fleet, it was clear that diesel traction would be suitable for both main line and secondary route operation. Until that time, only engines of 1,600 hp had been built and tested and, although they had coped with heavy trains and long runs, they had been working at full – or nearly full – capacity, and that was leading to excessive wear. Double heading these trains would have eased these problems and, although both engines could be operated by one man, the cost of this was prohibitive. The Committee had been assured though that a single 2,000 hp engine was being developed in this country that could fit within the loading gauge, and that this would solve any lack of power issues. This was 10203, being built at Brighton. 10101/2 had been built at Ashford.

The Committee listed the advantages of diesel traction along with the drawbacks. Advantages included not being reliant on an outside source for power, better acceleration and sustained power on gradients, and being able to work in either direction. One design of loco could be built with different gears to enable them to be used on express passenger services or heavy freight trains. The elimination of smoke would be a benefit to passengers and staff alike. Disadvantages included the question of availability of oil in the long term, and the fact that, until then, it had not been possible to install steam heating boilers due to lack of space, so long haul expresses could not be operated during winter months. Taking away one cab would allow a boiler to be installed, but this would negate the advantage of quicker turn round times at termini. Special heating vans could be built, but this would be expensive. The Committee were assured that 10203 under construction would include train-heating facilities, which would solve the problem. The cost of building this locomotive was £90,000. This was around four times as much as a Britannia 4-6-2, so any savings in running costs would have to be substantial to overcome this high initial outlay, and the union resistance to not having a second man in cabs was not helping these potential savings.

Comparisons were made in running costs per mile to run an express from Euston to Glasgow. These figures accounted for the fact that two 1,600 hp diesels would be needed to operate this service. It also took into account initial build costs. Steam emerged by far as the most economical, with figures of 58*d* (old pence) per mile, compared to 122*d* for diesels – even assuming having only one man in the cab. A similar study was made looking at freight services around the Oxford area and, although the gap was smaller, steam still worked out cheaper at 79*d* compared to 87*d*. Both steam and diesels were deemed to have a life expectancy of thirty years.

If reliable 2,000 hp diesels could be produced, this would reduce costs drastically. If dieselisation was to occur, the Commission recommended that it should not just be introduced for certain trips in an area, but for all services, so that maintenance costs would not have to be split over two forms of traction.

New maintenance workshops would have to be built – ideally away from the smoke and grime of steam sheds. Works large enough to operate economically could mean long distances running dead to and from the tracks they were using. However, it was stated that if more diesel multiple units and electric locomotives were built then they could share facilities, and more depots could be built as steam maintenance sheds declined.

Sixty-two diesel shunters had been taken over by the Railway Executive in 1948 – many from the LMS – and these were proving to be more economical than steam. More 350 hp locos had been ordered, and, when all had been delivered, there would be a total of 214 around the country. A larger 500/600 hp diesel mechanical shunter had been developed by the Southern and was undergoing trials, but was proving to be too slow when on main lines. Build costs were substantially lower than diesel/electric shunters built by other regions.

Diesel shunters had many advantages over steam when shunting. Shunters could be driven from either side, one man operation was possible, and this man had better views in either direction due to lack of smoke and side tanks. Diesels could also work for up to a week before maintenance was required, and they could be ready to work at a moment's notice.

More comparisons were made with twenty-four hours of shunting at Toton yard being used as the criteria for calculating costs. Steam came out as 307d per hour compared to 181d for diesel.

Initial outlay for a diesel/electric shunter was still expensive – £21,000 compared to £6,000 for a 0-6-0T – but the Committee were assured that these initial costs would fall if mass production was to come about.

Another sphere where steam was coming under pressure was the operation of diesel railcars. Although their use had been more widespread on the Continent, the GWR had limited experience with them. The Committee concluded that with faster turn round time at termini and one man operation, they would be more economic on secondary and branch lines. They also thought that the sight of modern, clean trains would help restore the public's confidence in the railway. It was also considered that they would be ideal for social clubs and societies to hire, in competition with the motor coach.

The Committee came to the following conclusions after their deliberations. Firstly, electrification of the network would entail a vast amount in capital outlay, and this was not affordable at the time as the country was still rebuilding after the war. Secondly, when it came to diesels, it was felt that there was no future for main line diesels unless 2,000 hp units could be successfully developed. If this was the case, then an area should be selected for a trial, where main line services were converted, with secondary routes operated by railcars and marshalling yards by diesel shunters – in such a way that maintenance costs could be spread and assessed. The Committee saw a bright future for railcars and set up an immediate investigation into which branch/secondary lines would benefit from changing from steam.

On considering steam it was noted that on the Southern, due to the advent of electrification, between 1929 and 1939 only an average of nine new locos were introduced each year. They recognised the fact that steam traction would remain the largest source of motive power for many years to come, but realised that there were no new innovations on the horizon that would stop the advent of diesel and electric locomotives in the future.

Fuel Shortages

The whole country was experiencing fuel shortages and many services had been suspended. The Down ACE was one service affected as were some of the Basingstoke semi-fasts. The Chard branch had lost its service for a while, with no services by the WR or the SR from Creech Junction or Chard Junction, but these were restored in July. Later in the year some services were reinstated, including most of the Western Section routes.

Accident

On 5 August, an accident occurred at Ford Station when the 11:17 Brighton to Portsmouth train ran past a home signal at danger, and collided with the 10:47 Three Bridges to Bognor service standing in the loop platform. Eight passengers and the motorman on the Portsmouth service were killed. Forty-seven others were injured, with a further forty requiring hospital treatment.

The leading carriage of the Portsmouth train telescoped into the rear of the Bognor train, to a distance of around 40 feet.

Both trains were made up of 2-BIL units, built in 1937, and were of steel panels on a wooden framework, mounted on a steel underframe. It was noted by the subsequent inquiry that the new stock being built was of an all-steel construction, and would have stood up to the impact better. But as there was so many older units still in service, their early replacement was not an option. Units 2100 and 2069 were severely damaged, with only slight damage being sustained by 2029/52.

While the track was blocked, services from Brighton were diverted to Littlehampton while Barnham was used as a temporary terminus for those services coming from the west. Buses were laid on to take passengers between the two. Breakdown cranes from Brighton and Fratton were used to clear the scene. Remarkably, the up line was open by 17:45, and both lines were opened by 19:50.

The inquiry concluded that the accident was caused by the incoming train overrunning the home signal at danger, but as the poor motorman was killed, the exact reason why would never be known.

Pullman Cars

In 1951, the British Transport Commission purchased all the stock from the Pullman Car Co. Mr Nabarro MP was not pleased with this and asked the Transport Minister – Mr Lennox-Boyd – to give direction to the BTC not to go ahead with the purchase. The minister replied that he had no power to do this. The MP for Brighton – Mr Teeling – said, 'My constituents will be horrified that this is happening because they do not wish to see the nationalised railways taking over something that has up until now been so efficiently run.'

However, the shareholders of the Pullman Car Co. voted in favour of the change of ownership – partly because the contract with the railways was due to expire in 1962 with no certainty that it would be renewed.

Seven new Pullmans were built at the Birmingham Railway Carriage & Wagon Co. at Smethwick for use on the Golden Arrow. They had in fact been started in 1938 for use on the LNER, but the war had intervened. This accounts for the fact that the Pullmans had Gresley designed bogies. There were four parlour cars – *Cygnus*, *Hercules*, *Perseus* and *Pegasus* (*Pegasus* also contained a Trianon bar) – and three kitchen cars, which were *Aquila*, *Orion* and *Carina*. Three more Pullmans were refurbished at Brighton Works. These were *Minerva* (brake/parlour), *Car 35* (parlour) and *Car 208* (brake/parlour). *Car 303* was also built at Brighton in 1952 and started life on the Devon Belle, which, following a spell out of our region, returned to work on the Bournemouth Belle.

Competition from Road Transport

In 1933 the Road and Rail Traffic Act regulated freight carried by road. There were three different types of licence available:

'A' licence – This was awarded to general hauliers.
'B' licence – This was awarded to general hauliers and manufacturers carrying their own goods.
'C' licence – This was awarded to those who only carried their own manufactured goods.

The Transport Act of 1947 limited holders of 'A' and 'B' licences to operating within 25 miles of their base. The holders of 'C' licences campaigned successfully against their restrictions and were exempt from the regulations. By 1951, 3,700 haulage businesses had passed into the control of the BTC and became known as the 'British Road Services'.

New Locos and Multiple Units

Brighton Works were kept busy building new locomotives, with the last of the West Country/Battle of Britain class 34110 *66 Squadron* being produced, as well as the last LMS 2-6-4Ts – 42079 to 95 – followed by BR 2-6-4Ts 80010 to 21.

10201 left Ashford on 4 January and went to Derby. 10202 emerged from Ashford Works and, during August, was trialled on seven- and eight-coach trains, before being sent to Nine Elms for staff training – prior to being used on Waterloo–Exeter services.

The first of the 4EPB units was completed at Eastleigh works. It was numbered 5001. The class was designed by Bulleid and used the underframes from redundant EMUs. They were to continue being made until 1957, by which time a total of 213 four-car sets would be produced. They were similar to the last batch of 4-SUBS, but the cab had been redesigned. Route indicators were now on a roller blind and they had a new style of buckeye automatic couplers. They derived their names from the electro-pneumatic brakes that were fitted to them.

Loco Movements

70014 *Iron Duke* was rostered on Eastern Section Continental workings and had needed the assistance of a Schools on one occasion at Tonbridge.

A special first-class Pullman train was run to Eastbourne on 1 March to take delegates to the Dollar Exports Convention. It returned two days later. It was in the hands of electric locomotive 20001 in both directions with 34038 in reserve for the outward journey and 42080 for the return trip. They weren't required but early in May it failed on at least a couple of occasions when working Newhaven boat trains, and had to be rescued by steam locos.

The first recorded ex-GWR Castle arrived at Bournemouth on an excursion from Worcester on Sunday 3 June. It was 4082 *Windsor Castle*.

The seventeen WD 2-8-0s that had been allocated to Bricklayers Arms, Redhill, and Hither Green, had been transferred back to the LMR by September.

End of Classes

The year saw the final examples of Billington's B4, 4-4-0 being withdrawn along with Stroudley's D1 0-4-2T, Marsh's I1X, 4-4-2T and J1 4-6-2T, Drummond's K10, 4-4-0 and T14, 4-6-0, Kirtley's T 0-6-0T, Wainwright's J 0-6-4T and Adam's T1, 0-4-4T.

Facts and Figures

£34.9 million profit was made over the course of the year, an increase of £8 million on the previous year.

Just over 1 billion passenger journeys were made in 1951 on the 24,000 passenger trains that ran daily. Clapham Junction had two claims to fame – not only was it the busiest station for trains with over 2,500 every day, it was also the largest covering nearly 28 acres.

The year saw nearly 500 fewer steam locos on the whole network, but twenty-three more electric locos and twenty more diesels. The most powerful locomotive in the country was the gas turbine engine 18000, producing 3,500 hp.

The number of wagons had increased during the year by 4,500 to 1,109,233.

1951 saw the number of motor vehicles increase by 500, and the number of horses drop by 1,500.

Miscellanea

The Thanet Belle was renamed the Kentish Belle.

The inaugural run of the Royal Wessex was made on 3 May with 34105 *Swanage* in charge when it left Weymouth at 7:38 a.m. The corresponding Down train left Waterloo at 4:35 p.m. behind 34008 *Padstow*.

On 20 August, the up Royal Wessex stalled in Bincombe Tunnel and slipped backwards. The last two carriages got embedded in the sand drag at the catch points. These had to be detached and the rest of the train went on its way while they had to wait to be pulled out by a T9 coupled to a N15.

There was another incident on the approach to Bincombe Tunnel, when 35013 *Blue Funnel Line* slipped to a stop in heavy rain. The guard put the brakes on and walked back down the track to place detonators on the line. Due to a lack of communication, the driver restarted the train and dragged it through the tunnel with the brakes on and minus his guard! At Dorchester, passengers complained of a bad knocking, and the rear coach had to be detached suffering from 'square wheels'.

The June edition of the *Railway Observer* reported that Leader class 36001 had been scrapped after being given very fair trials and test runs to prove itself. During May, two others stored at New Cross Gate were towed to Brighton for scrapping. 36003 became derailed when being pushed into the works, almost blocking the East Coast lines.

In June, Eastbourne hosted the 'International Union of Railways Conference', and an exhibition laid on in the goods yard hosted a variety of locos. Perhaps the most unusual was the Fell diesel 10100, which was towed to the town by Class 5 4-6-0 75000. Also on show were 70009 *Alfred the Great*, 73001, 20003 and shunter 15227.

The new oil refinery at Fawley was officially opened by the prime minister on 14 September and two special trains were run from London with circular boards over smokebox doors and coach roofboards suitably inscribed. 35013 worked from Waterloo to Brockenhurst while 34063 went to Southampton Central where M7s 30357 and 30375 worked the train forward to Fawley.

The Isle of Wight received its third new ferry since the end of the war; MV *Shanklin*, on the Portsmouth–Ryde route, delivered on 18 June. The other two were *Southsea* and *Brading*, which were screw driven and replaced paddle steamers.

On 21 October, 70004 *William Shakespeare* broke a connecting rod while working the up Golden Arrow. This was not the first failure of this sort in the class and resulted in the whole of the class being withdrawn for investigation.

1044 was an O1 still in Southern livery on 6 July 1951 after having been withdrawn the previous month. It started life as No. 44 in Ashford Works in December 1898.

On 6 July 1951, Wainwright's Class C 1271 was still waiting to receive its new BR number and lion on wheel crest. It had been built at Ashford in December 1904 and was withdrawn in July 1963.

Another 0-6-0, but this one of a later design being a 1938 Maunsell Southern Railway Q Class 30532 on 29 September 1951. It only lasted six months longer than the 'C' in the previous image, being withdrawn in January 1964.

Another class of 0-6-0 freight locos was the Class 700. These were designed by Drummond of the LSWR in 1897. This view of 30692 taken on 29 September 1951 shows how little protection from the elements the crews had. It was withdrawn in January 1962.

31809 was a U class 2-6-0 designed by Maunsell in 1928. It lasted nearly until the end of steam being withdrawn in January 1966.

Stewarts Lane was the setting for this shot of 31724, a C class engine designed by Wainwright for the SECR in 1900.

Bulleid's 1CO-CO1 when new and before any logos had been applied.

A freight train in the hands of ex-GWR 0-6-0PT 1367 makes its way along Weymouth Quay on 10 July 1951.

Chapter 3

1952

Derby Day

One of the greatest sporting occasions of any year is Derby Day, and that of 1952 was no exception, with the railways expected to carry thousands of extra passengers in over a hundred extra trains. Epsom Downs is the terminus of the branch from Sutton, although many racegoers alighted at Tattenham Corner, which is alongside the racecourse on a separate branch from Purley. Epsom Downs has eight platforms but only 3–7 inclusive are electrified.

To cope with the extra traffic, three extra sections were added controlled from three temporary signal boxes. They were known as 'A', 'B' and 'C' Intermediates. Signal arms were reattached to posts that were permanent fixtures, but not used for the rest of the year. Although Epsom Station opened at 5:00 a.m. as usual with only three staff, it was not long before the early racegoers started to arrive. At the height of the rush there were fifteen different grades of staff on duty to deal with a packed train arriving every few minutes. 660 Metropolitan Police even arrived by train. Extra signal, telegraph, and permanent way staff stood by – as did a breakdown gang – so as to minimise any delays should a problem occur.

Just over 100 trains arrived at the terminus that day – all made up of 2 × 4 car third-class suburban electric units. There was one first class Pullman special, which was pulled by electric loco 20003 that left Victoria at 12:35 p.m., returning at 5:40 p.m.

Centenary of Brighton Works

Brighton can thank the LBSCR's Chief Mechanical Engineer, J. C. Craven, for the decision to build a new locomotive works in the town. Until that time, the company had shared its workshops with its rival – the South Eastern Railway – at premises in New Cross. Until 1846 the two companies had shared a pool of locomotives, but this agreement came to an end and the stock of locos was shared out between the two companies. The premises at New Cross had become extremely cramped as services expanded, and J. Craven looked around for a site to build a new workshop. Brighton was the obvious choice, being central to all the company's services. New buildings were erected to the east of the station. These originally included the running shed, but it proved to be very difficult getting locos to and from their trains from this site. Together with the new premises becoming more cramped, it became obvious that a new running shed would need to be built elsewhere. Craven favoured an area of land between the western route and the main line to London. The problem with this was that the chalk that had been excavated to level the station site was piled high there and would have to be moved. Brighton Corporation objected to this, but when Craven threatened to move the works to another town, the council backed down. The chalk was eventually moved, being used to provide the embankments on the Steyning Branch.

In the early days of the works, the site was also used to make parts for the company's marine fleet, but this arm of its activities was eventually moved to Newhaven.

Craven retired in 1869. He had been renowned for building many small classes of engines that all used parts unique to them. This was causing long delays in the works as all parts had to be made specially. He was succeeded by William Stroudley, who set about rationalising the number of parts needed by designing new classes of engines that used interchangeable parts. On Stroudley's death in 1889, he was succeeded by R. J. Billinton, who carried on with the idea of using interchangeable parts. But, as his new designs were built, stocks of spares were needed for his and Stroudley's designs, creating more strain on the limited space within the works.

Billinton needed to expand the workshops but this was not easy as the premises were built on a hillside. He overcame this problem by building the extension on brick piers. Billinton succumbed to his failing health and he was succeeded in 1904 by D. Earle Marsh. Marsh designed a new boiler for his locos – the first class of which was the H1 4-4-2 – and also wanted to fit his boilers to his predecessor's designs. He built so many spare boilers that, when he came to build his E2 0-6-0 tanks, there were already enough boilers in stock. Space continued to be a problem within the works but Marsh solved this by moving the carriage works to Lancing and building another floor on top of part of the existing works. Another innovation introduced by Marsh was to convert the workshops to electrical power, thus making the old steam plant redundant. The original steam plant was an old Sharp boiler from an 1839 'single'. This had been replaced in 1909 by a vertical steam plant. Marsh also suffered from ill health and retired in 1911, to be succeeded by R. J. Billinton's son, L. B. Billinton.

The outbreak of the First World War brought an end to any new developments, with the workshops then being used for war work. After the end of hostilities, there was a reluctance to invest in new steam designs as electrification of the main line was being considered. The last engine to leave the works was 4-6-4 tank *Remembrance*, named in memory of those of the company's staff who had lost their lives in the war.

In 1923, when the Southern Railway was formed, R. E. L. Maunsell was appointed as CME. He had been CME for the SECR, and consequently favoured their designs. Brighton was used to build some 2-6-4 tanks of his River class design, as well as rebuilding Marsh's I1 4-4-2 tanks to Maunsell's designs. They also built his 8 Z class 0-8-0Ts.

Upon electrification of the Brighton line, the Southern decided to close Brighton Works and move all maintenance and building to either Ashford of Eastleigh.

The Second World War came to Brighton's rescue as the works was reopened and all-new machinery had to be installed. O. V. S. Bulleid had taken over as CME in 1937, and the first engines to be built under his regime were his Q1s and three electric locos: 20001/2/3. Brighton then built ninety-three 2-8-0s to LMS design to work the heavy freights needed for the war effort.

After the end of hostilities, Brighton was responsible for assembling many of the 4-6-2 West Country/Battle of Britain class, although many of the parts were manufactured elsewhere.

In July 1947, the works produced its 1,000th locomotive. This was 21C164 *Fighter Command*.

Brighton was also responsible for building Bulleid's controversial 0-6-0 + 0-6-0 Leader class. Any development on this design ceased on nationalisation and Bulleid left to further his career in Ireland.

Brighton continued building locos with some LMR 2-6-4 tanks, which were the forerunners of the BR tanks of the same wheel arrangement and were also designed and built at Brighton.

To commemorate the centenary of the works a special excursion was run on 5 October. This all Pullman train left Victoria behind H2 Atlantic 32424, *Beachy Head*. At Brighton, a tour round the works and shed was included as well as two return trips to Kemp Town behind A1X 32636 – the oldest Southern engine – before returning to London behind 32424. The cost of this tour including Pullman supplement was 22s 6d – £1.12½!

In 1952 the works were still flourishing and they were looking forward to a bright future. Little did they know! Locomotive building stopped in 1957 when BR 2-6-4T 80154 was completed. The works closed in 1962 and was demolished in 1969.

Exhibition at Battersea

An exhibition of the latest types of freight wagons was held at Battersea. Over twenty different types of wagon were on show. British Railways had inherited over 1.2 million wagons in 1948, made up of 480 different types. This enormous range could not be sustained and it was intended to cut this down to 150. Sixty-five different types had already been produced. The most common type was for carrying coal and for this there were two types. One was a hopper capable of carrying 24.5 tons and the other had a flat bottom with four side and one end door. Both were made of welded steel.

Canterbury and Whitstable Railway

The last train over this line was run on Saturday 29 November behind R1 31010. Two brake vans were attached, crammed full of press from newspapers and TV. The train left Canterbury with loud blasts on the whistle and detonators being set off. At Whitstable Harbour a crowd of over a hundred were waiting with bunting and flags. The loco picked up the eight remaining trucks at the harbour and took on water via the fire hydrant by the harbourmaster's office. The train left at 1:00 p.m. to much cheering, with coal being thrown from the bunker to the throng. On arrival back at Canterbury it ran over another set of detonators.

Accidents

On Sunday 20 July 1952, the 3:24 p.m. Southampton Central to Waterloo was approaching Shawford near Winchester where the four main lines merge into two. A 4-6-0 Lord Nelson class 30854, *Howard of Effingham*, was approaching the junction at around 30 mph on the local line. The Up local home was at danger to give preference to a late running Southampton to Waterloo boat train that was on the up through line. Both the signals for the Up local and Up through were mounted on the same post. The driver was not too familiar with the section of track and said that smoke from his engine was partly obscuring the signal, and he mistook the Up through being off for the Up local. He only realised his mistake when, approaching the junction, he noticed the points were not set to join the main line but were instead headed towards a siding and sand drag. He applied the brakes but was too late. The engine entered the sand drag and toppled over down an embankment. The tender and leading coach followed it down the embankment, but stayed upright. There were no injuries. The following boat train was brought to a halt by a red flag being waved. Passengers were transferred from the train that had just crashed and they continued on their journey. It was found that the driver was solely to blame for the accident.

A more serious accident occurred at Guildford on 8 November at 10:34 p.m. Class 700 0-6-0 30693 had just come off shed and was travelling at around 5 mph while on the down Alton and heading for the up Main. It was hit by a 2-BIL 2133 at around 40 mph. The force of the impact pushed it back around 30 yards. The EMU had suffered brake failure coming down the 1:100 Pinks Hill and passed a distant and home signal, both set at danger. The motorman and one passenger were killed, with another thirty-seven being injured and six needing to be detained in hospital. The cause of the accident was found to be a fuse blowing on the compressor governor. There should still have been enough air in the reservoir to bring the train to a halt. If pressure had been dropping for a while with previous brake applications, this would have shown up on the Duplex gauge in the cab. The Westinghouse brakes were so reliable though that most motormen did not keep an eye on the gauge. It was also dark and the spotlights that were supposed to illuminate the gauges were not always focused correctly. As an outcome, it was recommended that a control governor be fitted to the braking system so that if air pressure were to drop, power would be cut to the traction motors.

Early in the morning at Hither Green on 18 December, a visiting Class N1 0-6-2T 69475 from the Eastern Region derailed in the up yard and overturned, blocking the exit. Two cranes were called for and the loco was re-railed early in the afternoon.

New Locomotives

Diesel electric shunters were built at Ashford and 2-6-4Ts at Brighton. By the end of November the latest to leave was 80051.

Loco Movements

Continental freight trains often with braked wagons were run several times daily between Dover and Southwark Depot, or other London yards. King Arthurs were often employed on them with a maximum load via Tonbridge of 425 tons. Pacifics were allowed 500 tons, while Class U 2-6-0s were restricted to 400 tons.

Black 5s were regularly seen on excursions to the Sussex coast, but unusually, in June, 2 ER B1s 61138-9 were seen at Brighton and Eastbourne, having taken over trains from Hitchin and Cambridge at Canonbury, North London.

By the end of 1952, all the Schools class had lost their Southern green livery and had been given a coat of lined black paint, rather than the Brunswick Green given to other express engines.

Guy Fawkes Night was celebrated in many towns in the 1950s with places like Lingfield, Edenbridge and Lewes having special trains laid on – whether steam or electric. Although a 2-6-2T or 2-6-4T was normally sufficient to handle these, one ten-coach train to Uckfield had West Country 34104 *Bere Alston* in charge.

70004 *William Shakespeare* was still working the Golden Arrow – usually working one return trip from London to Dover. Merchant Navy 35022 *Holland America Line*, based at Dover, was having a harder life – normally working two return trips to the capital, including the Night Ferry.

On Friday 21 November, Her Majesty The Queen visited her naval air stations at Lee-on-Solent and travelled on a train of Pullmans behind West Country 34011 *Tavistock*. Other West Country locos were standing by in case of failure and these were stationed at Waterloo, Woking, Basingstoke, Eastleigh, Fareham, Havant and Guildford. The Pullmans used were *Isle of Thanet*, *Aries*, *Phoenix* (for the Queen), *Orion* and *Minerva*. Up until this trip, T9 30119 had been used for royal train duties.

The last Class I3 left Brighton under its own steam on 6 December, bound for Ashford where it was to be cut up.

End of Classes

The last of Wainwright's 4-4-0 B1 Class were withdrawn along with Marsh's I3, 4-4-2Ts, Earle's C3, 0-6-0s and Drummond's L11, 4-4-0s.

Facts and Figures

The gap in receipts over expenditure continued to grow with a surplus of £39.6 million. Nearly £112 million was received in passenger receipts, although passenger journeys dropped to just under 1 billion on 24,000 daily train journeys. The fall in passenger numbers was put down to the lack of large exhibitions, like the Festival of Britain, and bad weather.

The transport of coal and coke was the next biggest money earner, with an income of over £101 million. Transportation of coal amounted to over 50 per cent of all freight carried, with 170 million tons out of a total of 284 million tons. 16,000 freight trains were run daily.

Steam locomotive stock over the whole system had dropped to 18,864, with electric locos rising to 58 and diesels to 211.

The number of horses owned by British Railways dropped dramatically by over 1,000 to 2,179, whereas the increase in motor vehicles was from only 339 to 14,720.

Miscellanea

Many platforms on the Southern (Eastern Section) were increased in length to take ten-coach, rather than eight-coach, trains. This was to ease rush hour congestion.

On the Isle of Wight, passenger and freight services were withdrawn from the Ventnor West branch on Monday 15 September, and the stations at Godshill, Whitwell, St Lawrence and Ventnor West were closed.

70004 *William Shakespeare* was looking very smart, as it should have been seeing as it was in charge of the famous Golden Arrow Pullman service from Victoria to Dover. It was pictured at the latter on 9 August 1952. The previous year it had been on show at the South Bank Exhibition.

41295 was photographed at Stewarts Lane on 21 June 1952. It was one of a batch of thirty ex-LMS Class 2 2-6-2 tanks allotted to the Southern Region.

Larger 4P 2-6-4 tanks were also assigned to the Southern for a while. 42070 was one of thirty-four to be allocated to Southern sheds in the 1950s. Pictured on 9 August 1952, it was allocated to Ramsgate (74B).

Unrebuilt Merchant Navy Class 35010 *Blue Star* prepares to leave Waterloo on the Bournemouth Belle on 23 November 1952.

On the same day as the previous image, the crew of 0395 Class 30577 pose for photos before pulling the first leg of the RCTS Bisley Tramway & North West Surrey Rail Tour.

Two more views of the same rail tour in completely different surroundings. (Above) The tour had arrived at Brookwood and (below) the tour had divided at Brookwood and Class M7, 30027 made two return journeys to Bisley. The station had opened in 1890 and closed in July of 1952. The first two coaches were a Sheppey articulated set. These were originally eight railmotors designed for the Sheppey Light Railway, but in 1914 the engines were removed and the coaches formed into articulated sets. The Sheppey Light Railway closed at the end of 1950. This set had been used on the Kensington–Clapham Junction route but did not return to these duties after the excursion. They went to Eastleigh the following day and from there they were taken to Lancing carriage works.

Wandsworth Common was the scene for Class C 0-6-0 31575, working a freight on 27 September 1952.

Norwood Junction based 0-6-0 Q Class 30539 rests between duties on 27 September 1952.

A Maunsell-designed Class U1 31639 rests on shed, possibly Norwood Junction, on 5 July 1952.

C Class 31244 takes on water at Tonbridge shed on 9 August 1952.

Class 700 0-6-0 30696 at an unknown location on 19 April 1952.

A very smart looking Class Q1 33015 on 9 August 1952 at an unknown location.

As part of the RCTS Brighton Works Centenary outing on 19 October 1952, the Kemp Town branch was traversed. Pictured at the terminus was A1X 32636, waiting to return to Brighton.

Having visited the works and Kemp Town, the enthusiasts headed back to London behind H2 32425 *Trevose Head*.

Class 700 0-6-0 30316 looking as if it has just been given a new coat of paint at Eastleigh on 1 May 1954. It still had another eight years of service to give, being withdrawn in Dec. 1962 aged sixty-five years.

In charge of another rail tour was 1881 Adams Class 0395 30577 at Eastleigh on a Railway Enthusiasts Club tour of Southampton Docks on 8 May 1954. This was the loco used on the Bisley tour in 1951.

Chapter 4

1953

Transport Act 1953

In July, the Minister of Transport announced in Parliament that, with the exception of London Transport, the various Executives of the British Transport Commission would not continue after September. Their powers would revert back to the Commission, whose size would be increased from nine to fifteen members. The railways would be run by the British Railways Board.

One of the major effects of the Bill was to put road transport back into private hands. When the British Transport Commission had been set up, all long distance hauliers had been nationalised and this Bill reversed that. A Road Haulage Dispersal Board was set up to oversee the re-privatisation of the fleet. When first submitted to Parliament the privatised road hauliers were told they would have to pay a levy to the railways but, as the Bill made its way through Parliament, this idea was dropped.

The British Road Services division of the BTC had been successful with trade increasing from £1.1 million in 1948 to £8.9 million in 1953.

Trial of DMUs

There were worrying moves afoot for steam enthusiasts. A start had been made on the Modernisation Plan's £500,000 programme to introduce diesel units in place of steam on some branch lines. Although the trials were not in the South, but in the West Riding of Yorkshire, any success there would have repercussions nearer home. It was foreseen that, if successful, the 2-car units would become standard throughout the country. The units would be capable of being driven from either end, powered by 125 hp bus engines mounted beneath the floor. Either one or two engines could be used depending on requirements. Seating would be of the bus type as well and each unit would contain a toilet and a guard's van.

Isle of Wight

Southern Region announced that they intended to close the Newport–Freshwater and Newport–Sandown branches within a year and Ryde–Cowes within five years. The Merstone–Ventnor West had just closed. These closures would leave the Ryde–Ventnor line as the sole remaining service.

The last green O2 on the Isle of Wight was being given a coat of black paint after being overhauled. The loco had fewer tracks to run on after its return to service though as the branches between Brading and Bembridge and Newport and Freshwater were closed on 21 September. The Central Transport Consultative Committee had recommended that the lines between Cowes, Newport, and Sandown should remain open for at least two more years, but suggested that as it was holiday makers that used the lines the fares be increased so any losses were wiped out or decreased substantially.

Accident

There was an accident at Guildford on 18 September when an 8-car electric unit on a trip from Waterloo failed to stop when entering a bay platform. It ran into the sand drag at about 25 mph where the body was ripped from the bogies. It then skidded over the platform and crashed through a wall before demolishing three offices, including the stationmaster's office. The assistant stationmaster was fatally injured and there were six other injured people. The bay platform was shut until midnight on 20 September when the electric units were recovered. They had been made in 1951 and, with the bodies being of all-steel construction, stood up well to the impact. They did not telescope and stayed upright.

The subsequent inquiry found the driver to be solely at fault as he had entered the station too fast. It was also thought that he panicked when the brakes did not work straight away, even though it takes a second or two for air pressure to build up. He tried to engage reverse and, although this would work with the steam engines he used to drive, it simply blew the fuses on electric units.

New Stock

By February, the first twenty-five Standard class 4 2-6-0s had been completed at Horwich Works and fifteen of the class 76005–76019 had been allocated to Eastleigh (71A). As more were completed, Salisbury (72B) was to be allotted three, 76027–76029, and Redhill (75B) also three – 76053–76055.

At Brighton twenty new 2-6-4Ts were due to be produced throughout the year, starting with 80059.

Nationally, in 1953, 208 new locomotives were built but 426 were withdrawn. The number of locos introduced was less than planned due to a shortage of steel. Another forty-one diesel-electric shunters were introduced, making a total of 242. There were also seven new electric locos introduced, making a total of sixty-five.

Five diesel shunters, 13010–13014, from a batch of twenty-five new locos were allotted to the Southern Region. These were allocated to Eastleigh. As more came off the production line, Hither Green, Norwood Junction, and Brighton also received allocations.

11,136 new carriages were put into service – 648 being built in BR's workshops and 485 by private contractors. This figure was only 2 per cent of the total stock with shortage of steel being a problem for coachbuilding as well.

40,820 new wagons were built – 13,407 from railway workshops and 27,413 from contractors – and 38,867 were withdrawn. This was from a total stock of 1.12 million.

Loco Movements

The 1 in 50 Bincombe Bank outside Weymouth was still proving challenging for locomotives and their crews. Over the August Bank Holiday, 76019 made two excursions to Weymouth and, on the first trip, had to be banked by a T9 – 30117 – and the following day with a load of eight coaches, Lord Nelson 30852 *Sir Walter Raleigh* was called upon to assist, but the pair made fairly light work of it reaching the summit at between 30/35 mph.

A Western Region 2-6-0 was left to its own devices with an eight-coach train and was down to walking pace when it finally reached the summit. Not so lucky was a West Country class that was required to stop at Upwey Wishing Well Halt to serve a gymkhana. It failed to restart and assistance had to be called for, causing delays to the following services.

Special trains for ramblers were a common sight on Sundays, with many leaving from Victoria bound for various parts of the Southern Region. They were well-patronised and the rake of corridor stock used often needed to be double-headed by unusual combinations. One such special saw two Drummond Class 700s, 30308 and 30693, taking over from U1 31904 at Guildford to take the train onwards.

The Merchant Navy class were temporarily withdrawn to have their axles examined and their duty of operating the Night Ferry had to be double-headed with a Schools 4-4-0 30912 *Downside* and L1 4-4-0 31755 deputising on one occasion. Locomotives were brought in from other regions to cover and these included ex-LNER V2s 60829 and 60893 and B1s 61133, 61192 and 61354.

On Whit Monday, the return trip from Hayling Island needed two of the diminutive A1X tanks as their train consisted of six fully laden coaches. Earlier that month a special had been run by the Stephenson Locomotive Society called the Portsmouth Special. Locomotives were lined up at Fratton shed for the benefit of photographers who could then choose to go on a trip to Hayling Island or travel over the Gosport–Fareham branch, which would shortly close to passenger traffic.

In March, 10201/2 were joined by the LMS 10000/1 to work West of England expresses, including the Bournemouth Belle.

Facts and Figures

The Minister stated that £1.25 million had been saved by closing branch lines over the entire network. This was in answer to criticisms that replacement bus services were not always substituted for these closed branch lines. He went on to outline the benefits of dieselisation of branch lines but stressed the high initial outlay. One of the casualties had been the passenger services on the Gravesend West branch that closed on 3 August.

Receipts for the year had remained static from the previous year at £12.2 million but expenditure had risen meaning the profits had fallen to £0.9 million. There were about 300 fewer steam engines over the system, with only seven more electric and forty-nine more diesels built to replace them.

Since nationalisation and the introduction of the Standard types of steam locomotives, with older, less-efficient classes consigned to breakers' yards, coal consumption had improved from 35.26 miles run per ton to 36.73. Breakdowns were less frequent as well with 31,000 miles being run between breakdowns compared to 17,500 post-war.

Miscellanea

The Coronation of Queen Elizabeth II resulted in many thousands of people wishing to visit London to join in the celebrations. Cheap day returns were made available between Friday 29 May and Wednesday 3 June. The railways laid on 1,338 extra trains to cope with the influx, with many of these being run by the Southern.

August saw industrial action of railway staff in France having a knock-on effect on Continental boat trains in this country. In a lull in the industrial action, an additional thirty-two boat trains were run in 22 hours. This led to many travellers being stranded in London, so rest and refreshment facilities were laid on at Victoria Station. The action worsened again and this led to many boat trains being cancelled.

The Southern was the first region to do away with horse-drawn vehicles but 1,221 still remained, with sixty being on the streets of London.

A national programme of repainting stations was under way and Dorchester, Southampton Central, Tonbridge, Victoria, and Waterloo were some that had been spruced up.

Approval was given in principle to extend the third rail electrification from Gillingham to Margate and Ramsgate, from Sevenoaks to Dover and Folkestone, and from Tonbridge to Hastings.

Unrebuilt Battle of Britain 34074 *46 Squadron* passes Bickley Junction on 8 August 1953 on an Up Continental boat train.

A variety of motive power at Vauxhall. A 4-Cor 3123 in the foreground on an Aldershot or Farnham service with a Std Class 5 73003 on an adjacent platform on 22 May 1953.

Eastleigh, on 30 May 1953, had a variety of locomotives on display as usual. From right to left are H15, 30524, Lord Nelson 30857 *Lord Howe*, and M7 30031.

The SLS ran a trip from Victoria to Portsmouth and Southsea on 3 May 1953 behind Class H2 32425 *Trevose Head*. The return leg was in the hands of T9 30718.

On the same day as the photo on p.51 the SLS ran another railtour from Gosport along the branch to Bishops Waltham and back to Havant where this photo was taken. It was operated by M7 30110 between two push-pull sets, 31 and 36.

Nine Elms turntable with N15 30781 *Sir Aglovale* on the LSWR overbridge type turntable. This did get replaced in later years.

Three R1s, 31154, 31340 and 31337, pull the 1.20 p.m. boat train out of Folkestone Harbour. Out of shot is another R1, 31107, on banking duties.

Britannia Class 70023 *Venus* waits to leave Waterloo with an express passenger train on 16 May 1953.

On the same date as the top photo, H16, a Urie designed 4-6-2T, 30516, is on empty coaching stock duties at Waterloo.

From one of the largest tanks to one of the smallest. 30589 was a C14 0-4-0T designed by Urie as a rebuild from a Drummond 2-2-0 motor train. Pictured at Eastleigh on 5 September 1953, it ended its working life as DS77 at Redbridge sleeper depot where it survived until 1959.

The station buildings still survive today as this photo was taken at Rolvenden on the Kent & East Sussex Railway, but the shed is now on the other side of the tracks. A1X 32678 and (below) O1 31065 were on shed on 12 December 1953.

Another shot of 31065, but this time earning its keep by working a passenger train from Headcorn Junction, although with a train consisting of only one coach it is not difficult to see why the line closed.

T9 30727 at Salisbury on a Portsmouth Harbour via Eastleigh service on 3 October 1953. In the background is 34002 *Salisbury*.

32151 was an E1 introduced in 1874 by Stroudley. Originally it was numbered 2151 and named *Helvetia*. It was one of the last to survive being withdrawn in October 1960 at the grand age of eighty.

The tanks on the previous page were built for the LBSCR but 31339 was an SER design by James Stirling. There were twenty-five built from 1888. They were possibly best known for their banking duties at Folkestone Harbour. 31339 was scrapped in June 1958.

Another tank to be seen on the Eastern Section of the region was Wainwright's 0-4-4T Class H, 31276. Introduced in 1906, it was spotted at Ashford on 29 September 1953. It was scrapped in February 1961.

T9s gained the nickname 'greyhounds' due to their free running capabilities. 30287 was seen at Eastleigh on 5 September 1953. They were designed by Drummond for the LSWR in 1899. It was originally coupled to a six-wheeled tender, but given an eight-wheeled one in December 1902. 30287 was scrapped in November 1959.

31621 was at Ashford shed on 26 September 1953. It was a Class U 2-6-0 designed by Maunsell. The early ones were rebuilds of the ill-fated River Class tanks. It lasted until June 1964.

The S15s were a development of the N15 and designed for mixed traffic work. 30823, seen at Eastleigh, was introduced in March 1927 and withdrawn in November 1964.

The most powerful class of 4-4-0s in Britain were the Schools Class. 30902 *Wellington* was spotted at Ashford on 26 September 1953.

By 1953 there were many new Standard types to be seen around the Region and Class 3 2-6-2T 82016 was on shed at Eastleigh on 5 September 1953.

On the same day as the previous image, Class 4 2-6-0 76019 was also on shed at Eastleigh.

An ancient survivor on 15 August 53 was D class 31746. It was a Wainwright design for the SER in 1901. Its days were numbered though, being withdrawn in December 1954.

Chapter 5

1954

Ferries

The British Transport Commission was not only responsible for running the railways, but for road and sea traffic as well. The commission had been happy to let the railway companies in which the various ports were situated be responsible for their ferry services. This meant that the Southern were responsible for ferry services from Dover and Folkestone to Calais and Boulogne, Newhaven to Dieppe, Southampton to St Malo, Weymouth to the Channel Islands, and the Isle of Wight ferries.

In 1954 a report was commissioned to be compiled by Sir David Watson into the future of the shipping services.

Financial figures solely for the Southern ports are not available, but the shipping services as a whole were profitable. 1948 had seen a figure of £3.1 million being made. In 1953 a profit of £950,726 was made, and this was the lowest figure since nationalisation. A currency restriction of £25 being taken from the country had a minor effect on trade, but the fall in profit was mainly due not to a drop in trade but depreciation; until then this had been low as the fleet was ageing, but as new vessels were being introduced, it was rising, with a significant effect on the bottom line. In 1954, the average age of cross-Channel ships was eighteen compared to thirteen in 1939. Ships were depreciated over twenty-five years.

In 1950, the SS *Brighton* was introduced on the Newhaven service. This was to replace the SS *Brighton V* that was lost during the Second World War. When it was displaced in 1964 by roll on/roll off car ferries, it found work on the Weymouth–Channel Islands service.

The Southampton – St Malo service received a new ship in 1951; the SS *Normannia*, built at a cost of £750,000. The following year, the first roll on/roll off ferry was introduced. This was the *Lord Warden* on the Dover–Boulogne route. In 1958, SNCF introduced the *Compiegne* and in 1959 the *Maid of Kent* entered service, resulting in three vessels on the route.

The Isle of Wight routes also received two new vessels during the 1950s – the *Shanklin* in 1951 and the *Lymington* in 1959.

Southampton was not proving to be that successful with ferry services on the St Malo service under competition from the boats from Newhaven and Dover. The Southern also decided to concentrate all their sailings to the Channel Islands from Weymouth.

Although the motor car was beginning to be a major competitor to the railways, this was not the case for shipping as more people wanted to go abroad, and the 1950s saw growth continue. By 1960, income had risen to £19.2 million – compared to £11.1 million in 1948 – with a profit of £3.9 million. Shipping remained profitable until 1974.

Pullman Services

The BTC had offered to buy the entire share capital of the Pullman Car Co. Ltd, and this offer was accepted by over 95 per cent of the shareholders. The company changed hands on 1 July. Their contract to run services on British Railway's tracks was due to expire in 1962 and, as there was no chance of an extension, the BTC's offer was seen as fair. In December 1881, the LBSCR had been the first railway to run an all Pullman train, and they achieved another first when they ran the first train to be lit by electric light. The BTC, which operated Pullmans through the Hotels Executive, vowed that there would be no alterations to any of the Pullman services run on the Southern.

Brighton Line Resignalling

Stage 3 of the Brighton Line resignalling programme was finished in March. This was the Norwood – Selhurst – East Croydon triangle.

Accident

On 13 February at 9:33 a.m. at Windmill Bridge Junction just north of East Croydon, a six-car electric train became derailed on a moveable diamond crossing. It was the 8:09 a.m. from Littlehampton to London Bridge. Around 100 passengers were on the train – four of whom complained of shock, but there were no other injuries as the train remained upright. The passengers were transferred to a local train at 10:06 a.m. Steam cranes were brought in from Nine Elms and Brighton and the carriages were removed that afternoon. The Down line from London Bridge was opened at 4:35 p.m. that day, but the Up line to London Bridge, and both Up and Down lines from Victoria, were not opened until Monday morning at 6:00 a.m., due to considerable damage to track and signalling. The driver of the train was found to be solely to blame as he had overrun a distant signal at caution and a home signal at danger. No reason was found for his mistake.

New Locos

In 1954, 10203 was built at Brighton. Although similar in design to 10201/2, it incorporated an uprated 2,000 hp engine. It joined the previous two at Nine Elms.

Standard Class 4 2-6-4Ts continued to be built at Brighton. Their entire output would eventually consist of 80010–53, 80059–105 and 80116–54.

The first of BR's Standard two-car EPB units appeared from Eastleigh Works. They numbered from 5701. They were to replace the 2SL and 2WIM units being used in the suburbs. There were EPBs already running on the system, but these were to Bulleid's design dating back to 1951. The two types looked quite similar, but Bulleid's design had a window over the door and the cabs were not accessed by a separate outside door, but rather via the vestibule.

Loco Movements

The immaculate condition of 70004 *William Shakespeare* came in for praise when it was operating the Golden Arrow.

Southern electric locomotives had been spotted working the Hastings to Birmingham trains. Portions from Eastbourne were attached at Polegate. They had also been seen in charge of the Hastings to Manchester service, hauling the trains as far as Brighton. These trips were fitted in between hauling the boat trains from Victoria to Newhaven and back.

In July it was noted that all five diesel electric locomotives – 10000/1 and 10201/2/3 – were working expresses out of Waterloo bound for Exeter or Weymouth. This included the Atlantic Coast Express, where 10203 had been seen at Salisbury with 7P/6F stencilled on the cab sides in the style of steam engines. 10202 also had a spell working the Golden Arrow and Night Ferry services between Victoria and Dover.

Later in the year, 10201/2 were reallocated to the LMR at Camden, with 10203 joining them the following year and regularly double heading the Royal Scot. They were found less and less work and had all been scrapped by the end of 1963.

End of the Class

Only one class became extinct during the year – the Class 0458. This consisted of 0-4-0ST *Ironside*, which worked on Southampton Docks.

Facts and Figures

1954 proved to slightly more profitable over the previous year, with a surplus of £1.1 million of receipts over expenses being made. Passenger services were stable, with over 1 billion journeys still being undertaken on 24,000 weekday services.

Over 73 million parcels were still transported, either having been picked up from the senders' homes or having been taken to the station. Only 553 horses remained to deliver these parcels while motor delivery vehicles numbered 15,668.

The railway's safety record had always been very good and in 1954 not a single passenger was killed in all the 20.712 billion passenger miles. The average since nationalisation was one death per 759 million passenger miles. This figure would have been much better if it did not have to include the 108 who lost their lives at Harrow and Wealdstone in 1952.

Ashford saw another veteran 0-6-0 in the shape of Class O1 31048 on 29 May 1954. It was built by Stirling as a Class O in December 1893 and rebuilt with new boiler in August 1908 by Wainwright. It was withdrawn in October 1960.

Continuing with views of 0-6-0s, here is C2X 32523 at Ashford on 29 May 1954. It was built by R. J. Billinton for the LBSCR in August 1900 and rebuilt with a new boiler in April 1924 by D. Earle Marsh. It lasted until February 1962.

Working hard on 14 November 1954 was ex-LMS 4P 42089 at Selsdon on a Down East Grinstead service.

Lord Nelson 4-6-0 30851 *Sir Francis Drake* in BR express passenger green livery on Eastleigh shed on 4 September 1954.

T9 30289 and Lord Nelson 30853 *Sir Richard Grenville* on shed at Eastleigh in 1954.

Looking resplendent on 24 October 1954 was Britannia Class 70004 *William Shakespeare* on the turntable at Dover, before heading the Up Golden Arrow.

Chapter 6

1955

British Transport Commission

On 1 January the Railways Division of the British Transport Commission came into effect. Answerable to them were six Area Boards. These boards coincided with the regions that already existed. The Railways Division would be responsible for matters that were common to all regions including design of future locomotives, rolling stock, signalling and permanent way.

The 'Modernisation and Re-Equipment Plan' was published by the BTC. It came up with five main areas of expenditure:

1.	Track improvements and colour light signals, with centralised traffic control and better telecommunications	£210 million
2.	Steam must be replaced rapidly by diesel and electric traction, with no new steam engines to be built after 1956	£345 million
3.	Steam hauled rolling stock to be replaced by EMUs and DMUs	£285 million
4.	Freight transport remodelled with many fewer marshalling yards. Larger freight wagons would be built with continuous brakes	£365 million
5.	Other expenditure	£35 million
	Total	£1.24 billion

The result of this expenditure was expected to be faster, cleaner, more frequent passenger services between large urban areas, with speeds of 100 mph being reached. Other services must be reasonably economic or transferred to roads.

Freight would be subject to complete reorganisation to speed up movements and reduce costs. A return of £85 million per annum was projected on the investment.

Despite the increase in car ownership, it was foreseen that the new improved services would attract more passengers. It was also envisaged that the railways would win back some of the goods traffic lost to road transport.

In the Southern Region, all routes east of a line from Reading to Portsmouth would be electrified as soon as circumstances would permit. This would entail electrifying

250 route miles at a cost of £25 million. With the introduction of EMUs and diesel hauled freight, this would eliminate steam from the entire area.

The report continued, saying that the greatest early advantage would be to eliminate steam on the Waterloo to Southampton, Bournemouth, Weymouth and Exeter services. It was realised that there were still 19,000 steam engines in service, many of them being of modern design, so the first ones to be withdrawn would be the older, less efficient types.

Many of the 42,000 steam hauled passenger carriages would need to be replaced by new diesel or electric multiple units. The only non-corridor coaches to survive would be on suburban routes, where the ability to board and alight quickly was essential.

When it came to consider freight traffic, it was realised that many of the marshalling yards dated back to when individual companies owned the railways, and that there were too many of them – often at inconvenient places – which led to freight journeys between yards being shorter and slower than necessary, and so fewer but larger yards were envisaged. These new yards would be laid out to 'provide the expeditious transfer of full-loads between road and rail'. The average speed of freight trains would have to be raised and this would be done by the fitting of continuous brakes. There were over 1,000 places on the entire system where trains had to be stopped to have the brakes pinned down and continuous brakes would eliminate the need to do this. In 1955 there were over 1.1 million wagons and there was clearly scope for reducing this fleet by using larger wagons, but it was realised that although it was far better to transport full wagon loads, this could not always be possible and many wagons would still be only partially full.

It was planned to build 255,000 new wagons by 1970, but with higher speeds and better turn round times by 1974 it was envisaged that the stock would fall to 752,000.

Completion of Colour Light Signalling

On Sunday 8 May, the final connection was made. This meant that the whole line between London and Brighton was then colour signalled. Earlier stages had been brought into operation in October 1950, October 1952 and March 1954. This section linked up from Gloucester Road to Victoria, which had been colour light operated since 1954, and Coulsdon to Brighton over twenty years earlier.

5,600 trains passed the area weekly. The signalling system allowed a headway of two-and-a-half minutes between trains. They were controlled by three signal boxes at East Croydon, South Croydon and Purley. They were of brick construction with concrete roofs and were centrally heated. The changeover meant that the lines were closed for around seven hours while over 120 signal arms and fittings were removed. 100 sets of points were disconnected from their old boxes and reconnected to the electric point machines that had previously been installed and tested. It took over 500 staff from the Signal Engineers Department, brought in from all over London.

Kempton Park Races

We saw earlier the problems caused by the crowds using the trains for the Derby at Epsom; similar problems were experienced with Easter Monday meetings at Kempton Park. The station was only open on race days and is on the Shepperton Branch, around a quarter of a mile east of Sunbury Station. The station has two island platforms capable of holding eight-coach trains, but has no electrified sidings. The usual thirty-minute service could not hope to cope with the influx and trains were scheduled to arrive every four minutes.

After disgorging their passengers they continued to Sunbury, where they switched to the Up line returning to Waterloo to pick up another load. Around noon, with most of the punters at the track, it was pointless returning to pick up any more and the units had to be stored ready for the homeward rush. The Signal Engineers then established single line working over the Down line between Shepperton and Sunbury, which the usual daytime service had to use. The extra units laid on had to be stored ready for the return rush. They was done by lining the units up as they left Sunbury, treating the Up line as a siding with the units stopping close to the one in front. They then awaited the call to move forward to Kempton Park to pick up the returning racegoers.

Accidents

At 7:45 p.m. on 25 January at Bournemouth Central, an H15 4-6-0 travelling from Weymouth to Waterloo on a passenger train collided with a Lord Nelson 4-6-0 that was coming off shed. The passenger train was travelling at around 20–25 mph as it entered the Up Local, hitting the light engine head-on but at an acute angle. Both engines suffered extensive damage and were derailed, as was the leading coach. Four crew and one passenger were injured but not seriously. Steam cranes were brought in from Eastleigh and Salisbury and all running lines were opened by 6:30 p.m. the following day, although trains continued to be hand-signalled until the damage to the signalling equipment could be fixed. The accident caused major operational problems as fifteen other locos were trapped on shed by the accident and the coaling and watering facilities could not be accessed. The accident was caused by the driver of the light engine mistaking a semaphore signal for his, when he was actually being controlled by a shunting signal which was at danger.

A serious accident occurred near Barnes at 11:28 p.m. on 2 December. The 11:12 p.m. four-coach electric service from Waterloo to Windsor and Chertsey ran into the back of a forty-two-wagon freight train hauled by an LMS 2-8-0 8F. The four-car electric units were made up of two two-car units; 1853 and 1877. These had been introduced in 1935/36, being built on new steel underframes, but using wooden bodies made around 1895 for steam hauled operation adapted to fit the new underframes. These units were travelling at around 35 mph when they smashed through the brake van and a container on the wagon in front before turning over. Electrical arcing started a small fire which quickly turned into a blaze. The guard on the goods train, the motorman, and eleven of his passengers all perished. Twenty more passengers were seriously injured while another twenty-one suffered minor injuries or shock.

The few remaining services that night were diverted or stopped short, with London Transport supplying buses to cover the closed section. Normal services were resumed the following day at 5:48 p.m. after the wreckage had been cleared and the track and signalling systems repaired. The subsequent inquiry found that the freight train had been travelling slowly after being stopped at Barnes Junction Local home signal. The electric unit had entered Point Pleasant Junction section under clear signals and the accident had then been caused by irregular operation of the Sykes lock and block apparatus. The signalman at Barnes Junction was found to be solely to blame. The details of the signalling system are too lengthy to go into here but can be found in the official report.

Another accident occurred on 23 December at 8:29 p.m. when a Waterloo–Portsmouth electric train was hit in the rear by a slow moving steam train on a Waterloo–Basingstoke service. The rear of the EMU was crushed and ripped from its rear bogie, which was pushed towards the adjacent Up line. A passing electric unit then hit this, receiving superficial damage but staying on the tracks. The guard and twenty-one passengers were slightly injured. Power, which had been cut off following the collision, was restored to the Up/Down Local lines that had not been affected at 10:15 p.m. The wreckage was cleared overnight and all four running rails were operational by 8:00 a.m. the following morning.

The cause of the accident was found to be due to the driver of the steam engine having mistaken a bright distant signal for the Local line to be for his Through line. This was partly because this amber light was brighter than the Through red light, which made it difficult to see.

New Locos

BR Standard Class 4s and Class 5s continued to be delivered throughout the year, with Stewarts Lane and Eastleigh being two sheds to receive allocations.

New EPB units continued to be completed at Eastleigh.

It was officially announced that new six-car diesel units would be built for the Hastings line.

Loco Movements

Diesel electric 10203 was transferred to the LMR.

An unusual sight at Eastbourne was the use of a 700 0-6-0 on two inter-regional excursions. 30306 first worked from Hastings to Eastbourne on the 10:45 Hastings–Walsall ten-coach train, before returning to Hastings at the head of a train from Northampton. H2 Atlantics were regularly used on excursions from the south coast at the time.

Although the new Std 5s had relieved the pressure on the busy Victoria to Kent coast services, aging D1s and E1s could still be seen on express services.

End of Classes

The year saw the demise of the last of Billinton's D3 0-4-4Ts as well as Wainwright's E Class 4-4-0s.

Facts and Figures

The railways had a good year financially, with a profit of £2 million being made – the best since 1948.

The number of steam engines had declined by 465 over the year to 17,955, with 153 new diesel shunters being built to replace them.

Horses employed on roads and goods yards dropped by 230 to 323. Freight transported fell by 1.4 million tons, whereas parcels carried rose by around 400,000 to 153.2 million.

Under the 'Modernisation Plan', it was envisaged that 20,000 new coaches would be built over the next seven years. These would replace 25,000 coaches, including all 14,000 wooden-bodied ones. 7,700 of these would be loco hauled coaches, the remainder being diesel or electric multiple unit stock.

Miscellanea

The track between Headcorn and Tenterden on the KESR was removed by Messrs Cohens. They started around a quarter of a mile outside Tenterden Town Station. Biddenden goods yard was used as a depot for unloading materials, which were then removed by road. An Ashford O1 was always used for this work. At Rolvenden, the engine shed and station buildings were demolished.

The 2.5-mile-long branch line to Tidworth was opened in 1901 to carry military personnel from Ludgershall to the army camp at Tidworth on Salisbury Plain. It had opened to the public in 1902, but on 19 September it closed and the line passed to the War Department, finally fully closing in 1963.

ASLEF, the train drivers' union, went on strike from 29 May until 14 June over pay. The strike brought British industry to a virtual standstill until Eden's Conservative government gave in and paid the drivers. This did have a long term negative effect though, as government policy then became to switch more freight and passenger traffic to the roads.

The BR steam ship *Worthing* was sold to Greece and renamed *Phyrni*. It had been launched in 1928 and used on the Newhaven–Dieppe service, except for during the war when she was used as a hospital ship.

The Gypsum mines near Robertsbridge were a significant source of freight in the region, with 400,000 tons being produced every day needing 140 wagons to take it away.

U 31612 entering Betchworth Station on 16 July 1955 at the head of a Redhill–Reading service.

The short wheelbase made the P class engines ideal for shunting in confined spaces, such as here at Dover docks. 31027 was on duty on 14 July 1955.

Also working at Dover on the same day as the previous image was B4 0-4-0 30084.

At the other end of the size spectrum to the previous image is Merchant Navy 35010 *Blue Star*, taking water on 13 July 1955.

More water is taken on, this time by M7 30054 at Alton on 29 January 1955.

Class 0298 30587 on the turntable at Amesbury. It was normally used on china clay trains from Wenford Bridge but on 15 May 1955 it headed an excursion from Andover Junction to Bulford Camp.

On Whit Monday, 30 May 1955, there was a rail strike, but this train still managed to run. It was the 09:15 Charing Cross to Dover and Deal, hauled by 30909 *St Pauls*. The roof board on the leading carriage read 'Continental Express'.

Feltham hosted two different locos on 21 May 1955. To the left was Class 0395 30568, while on the right stood H16 30517.

A modern-looking Surbiton on 11 April 1955 was a good place to be trainspotting. Above Merchant Navy 35008 *Orient Line* and below N15 30452 *Sir Meliagrance* both pass through, bound for Waterloo from the South Coast.

On 6 February 1955 the RCTS ran a rail tour called The Hampshireman. It ran from Waterloo to Guildford, Horsham, Petersfield, Farnborough and back to Waterloo. Above, a pair of E5Xs – 32576 and 32570 – prepare to leave Guildford, while below T9s 30301 and 30732 are at West Meon on the return leg.

Four views of Clapham Junction on 30 July 1955, starting with N Class 31812 heading south towards the Sussex Coast.

A Class H2 32421 *South Foreland* heads a passenger service, possibly to Newhaven Harbour, which was a regular turn for these 4-4-2 locos.

Travelling north and heading for the West London line via Kensington Olympia and Willesden Junction was Black 5 45146 on an inter-regional working.

A week later but still at Clapham Junction, C2X 32445 was spotted.

On 15 May 1955, T9 30719 headed a Ramblers Excursion, the 'William Penn Special', from Waterloo to Great Missenden. Here it was passing under the old Clapham signal box that collapsed on 10 May 1965, causing widespread disruption.

The headcode would suggest that ex-LMS 4P 42074 was on a Victoria to Tunbridge Wells West service when photographed on 20 August 1955.

'The Wealden Limited' was an RCTS rail tour on 14 August 1955. Here, H 31177 double heads with O1 31048 at Goudhurst. The tour ran from London to Hawkhurst, then on to Hastings, returning via Polegate, Lewes and Horsted Keynes. The tour had originally been planned for 12 June, the day after the closure of the East Grinstead–Lewes line, but the ASLEF strike meant it had to be postponed.

Ashford was the scene where a very clean C 31298 stands in front of an equally clean double-domed C2X 32551 on 7 May 1955.

The fireman rearranges his coal on Std 5 73082 at Stewarts Lane. This engine was later named *Camelot*, escaped the cutter's torch, and is currently working on the Bluebell Railway.

Q1 33022 was at an unknown location when snapped pulling a train of bogie hopper wagons on 16 July 1955.

Chapter 7

1956

4-CEP/4-BEP

With the extension of electrification of more lines in Kent, and with the existing EMU fleet becoming more aged, there was an urgent need for more electric trains. These came in the shape of 4-CEP (corridor electro-pneumatic) and 4-BEP (buffet electro-pneumatic) units.

They were based on the standard BR Mk1 carriage design and using many electrical components of the EPB units. The cab ends were simply the ends of Mk1 stock but with cab windows, headcode boxes, and control connections added.

There were initially four prototype 4-CEP (7101–4) and two 4-BEP (7001/2) units built at Eastleigh for use on the Kent Coast and Central Sussex services, and these were trialled on the Central Division to and from Brighton. They were given a fairly robust trial with a twelve-car train made up of two 4-CEP and one 4-BEP being on a running that started from Eastbourne at 6:47 a.m. heading for London Bridge, then to East Croydon, Victoria, Brighton, Victoria and Streatham (layover), then to London Bridge, Littlehampton and West Worthing (layover), before returning to Eastbourne, where it was berthed overnight.

After the prototypes, forty-eight more units were ordered (7105–7153) with another fifty-seven (7154–7211) being ordered later. It would be 1963 before the last one was delivered. They proved to be very successful, becoming the longest serving EMUs, with the oldest surviving for forty-nine years, and the last one disappearing from the network in 2005.

Nationally, during 1956, a total of 435 electric multiple unit carriages and 275 diesel multiple unit carriages were produced. These were still in a minority, as a total of 1,950 carriages of all descriptions were produced. At the end of the year there were 41,522 passenger coaches in service, which was a reduction of 1,200 at nationalisation.

2-HAP Units

Thirty-six new units were started using the underframes from withdrawn 2-NOL (no lavatory) units. They were designated 2-HAPs (half lavatory electro-pneumatic) and were to be used on semi-fast and suburban services. These were numbered 5601–36.

Another batch of all new 2-HAPs were also ordered. There would be 173 of these units produced over the next few years, being numbered 6001–6173. They all looked identical from the outside but the layouts of the passenger compartments had some differences. They could be seen over all three sections of the Southern.

Abolition of 'Third Class'

From 3 June, 'Third Class' travel was abolished, with 'First' and 'Second' becoming the only classes available. This change coincided with the rest of Europe bringing in the same system. Until that time, 'Second Class' had only been available on Continental boat trains, so in effect it was actually 'Second Class' travel that was being abandoned, with 'Third' just being rebranded. It was also decided at the time to only have numbers or labels on the outside of 'First Class' compartments.

Accidents

On 22 October, two electric trains collided just outside London Bridge Station. The accident occurred at 8:31 p.m., causing injuries to four crew and fifteen passengers. A track circuit had failed and services had to be hand signalled. An instruction from the signalman to release the 8:15 from Platform 20 had been misunderstood and the 8:24 to Horsham had been signalled away from Platform 19 instead. The message had been given to a porter who relayed it to the station foreman. The Horsham train travelled around 500 yards when it struck an incoming service at an angle on a crossover. The accident would have been worse had both motormen not realised they were on a collision course and braked hard. Passengers had to climb down from the units onto the track and be escorted back to the station. Both units stayed upright on the track and were cleared away quickly, allowing the lines to be fully reopened by 3:30 a.m. the following morning.

Another accident occurred at 6:33 p.m. on 22 November, which could have had more serious consequences than it did. The 5:37 p.m. Waterloo–Ascot via Woking was made up of four two-car electric units. While travelling between Brookwood and Farnborough the last coach became derailed by a broken rail. The derailment broke a brake line, which brought the train to a halt. The coach stayed upright but lurched towards the adjacent Down line. The guard went back up the track waving his red lamp, which was spotted by the driver of the approaching 6:00 p.m. Waterloo–Plymouth steam hauled service, who made an emergency brake application. He did not stop in time but the damage to both trains was slight. The Plymouth service carried on its way and so did the electric units after the last two carriages had become detached. A full service was back in operation by 8:25 a.m. the following morning, after the track had been fixed.

New Locos

A total of 153 new diesels had been introduced during the year, making a final count of 609 – the vast majority of which were shunters, with main line diesels still being in the experimental stage. The number of electric locos remained constant at seventy-one.

In January it was reported that Std Class 5s 73110–9 had been allocated to Nine Elms. Class 4s 75070–9 had been allocated to Exmouth Junction, although their stay was short lived as they were soon moved to Bath Green Park, Eastleigh and Basingstoke.

A total of 663 Standard types locomotives had been introduced nationally by the end of the year, including 140 2-10-0 heavy freight locos.

Loco Movements

In February, A1X 32670 was sent to Dover Docks to rescue B4 30084 that had failed.

Royal trains were in the hands of Schools, with 30927 *Clifton* in charge of a Pullman train transporting the Queen Mother from London to Wye. In July 30906 *Sherbourne* disgraced itself by breaking down at Vauxhall when backing up to the royal train that was taking the Queen from Waterloo to Southampton. 30907 *Dulwich*, which was standing by at Nine Elms, was hurriedly called upon and the train left on time.

Throughout the year, Eastleigh was turning out rebuilt Merchant Navys. 35015 *Rotterdam Lloyd* was the first rebuilt Merchant Navy to run on the Eastern Section after returning to its home shed, Stewarts Lane.

73087 and 73088 were working out of Bath on the Somerset and Dorset line.

Bognor saw a lot of inter-regional excursions during the summer, but locomotives could not work through as the shed had been demolished during the summer and there was no longer any coaling facilities. West Countries were in charge of most of these.

Last of the Class

1956 saw the end of the two Hawthorn Leslie 0757 0-6-2Ts, Wainwright's D, 4-4-0s and R1 0-4-4Ts, Drummond's D15,4-4-0s and Billinton's E5 0-6-2Ts.

Facts and Figures

Despite the fact that the number of steam engines was diminishing, they were still using nearly 13 million tons of coal annually. This kept 44,000 miners employed. 70 per cent of all coal mined was moved from the pits by rail.

For the first time since nationalisation, the railways spent more than they earned. Receipts were only £480 million compared with £496.6 million expenses meaning a working loss of £16.6 million was incurred.

Over 1 billion passenger journeys were still being made, although the number of trains being run daily had dropped to 23,000.

The railways' shipping services were still proving to be profitable with a surplus of £1.8 million receipts over expenditure being recorded. If you were a horse, the future was not looking good as only 200 were left working for the railways. This was down from 7,600 at nationalisation. Motor vehicles had increased from 12,300 to 15,800 over the same period.

The failure rate of locomotives continued to improve with the introduction of the Standard designs, and figures for 1956 showed only one failure every 45,000 miles.

Miscellanea

Work had started on a new goods depot at Crawley.

There was a 'Clean Air Act' of 1956, which gave local authorities the right to restrict or stop emissions from buildings. This did not did not affect the railways on its inception, but there were provisions within the Act that dealt with dark smoke, grit, and dust from industrial chimneys that could have had an impact in the future.

The BTC announced that, in future, all freight wagons would be fitted with vacuum brakes. The fitting of continuous brakes would allow freight trains to run at nearer to express train speeds. Older stock was also being converted. Nearly 60,000 new wagons were introduced in 1957, of which 33,000 were all-steel mineral wagons. Bigger wagons were also being introduced, with 4,500 hopper wagons with a 21-ton carrying capacity, as well as 1,300 iron ore wagons with 25-ton capacity, and 534 33-ton capacity, being produced. Container traffic was also increasing, with 40,000 in service and authorisation to build another 13,000 over the next two years being granted.

E4 0-6-2T 32497 was a R. J. Billinton design for the LBSCR introduced in 1900. It was originally numbered 497 and named *Dennington*. This was in fact a spelling mistake and in 1905 it was renamed *Donnington*. Photographed at Nine Elms on 26 May 1956. It was withdrawn in November 1959.

A study in Urie 4-6-0s. Above, an N15 King Arthur, 30747 *Elaine* – an express loco with 6-foot 7-inch driving wheels and eight-wheeled tender – and below, a H15, 30482 – a mixed traffic engine with 6-foot driving wheels coupled to a six-wheeled tender. Both seen at Nine Elms shed on 26 May 1956.

Drummond designed the 0-4-4T M7 for the LSWR in 1897. There were 105 in the class that took fourteen years to introduce, with design alterations made along the way. 30124 was one of the earlier examples being introduced in February 1903. Seen here at Nine Elms on 26 May 1955. It was withdrawn in May 1961.

The most powerful 4-4-0s in the country were the Class V or Schools. 30914 *Eastbourne* was pictured at Stewarts lane on 26 May 1956. They were built for the Hastings line so had to fit within the restricted loading gauge.

Southern's most powerful locomotives were the Merchant Navy class. 35020 *Bibby Line* is shown at Nine Elms on 26 May 1956.

2-NOL 1825 enters Holland Road Halt on a Brighton–Worthing service on 17 March 1956. (Courtesy Edwin Wilmshurst)

30032, an M7, was on an Alton–Winchester passenger service on 2 April 1956. It was photographed just outside Alton.

7103 was one of the original 4-CEP units delivered in 1956 and allocated to Brighton for trials before being moved to services in Kent. They were the first EMUs built to Mk1 coach design.

7103 heads 7102 and 7101 through Haywards Heath on 15 July 1856 with the 11:08 Brighton to Victoria. (Courtesy Charlie Verrall)

20002 at Wivelsfield with the 09:05 Victoria to Newhaven Harbour service on 16 June 1956. (Courtesy Charlie Verrall)

Merchant Navy 35018 *British India Line* with the Down Atlantic Coast Express at Salisbury on 21 June 1956. (Courtesy Charlie Verrall)

Chapter 8

1957

Cannon Street Signal Box Fire

On 5 April there was a disastrous fire that destroyed the signal box at Cannon Street. It was a two-storey Westinghouse Brake & Saxby Signal Co. Ltd 'K'-style box, housing 143 miniature power levers. The fire broke out on the ground floor, caused by a short circuit in the wiring. The fire caused the station to be closed completely for three days and partially for four weeks.

Some electric trains could still use Cannon Street, but all steam services were diverted to Victoria or terminated at Sevenoaks or Tonbridge.

A temporary box was rebuilt on the ground floor of the refurbished fire-damaged box. A second temporary box, which was operational from 5 May, was housed in the Porters' Room. A new box was commissioned on 15 December and this was used until April 1976, when its operation was taken over by the London Bridge signalling scheme.

DMUs for Hampshire

In September, a fleet of eighteen two-car diesel electric multiple units were introduced. They were numbered 1101–1118 and became known as Hampshire units as they worked services from Portsmouth to Salisbury, Southampton, Eastleigh, Winchester and Alton. They used the same engines and electrical equipment as the six-car units on the Hastings line, but only had one engine per unit as opposed to two on the latter. The introduction of the units led to improved timetables being introduced for the winter period. The following year, four more units were introduced to run on branch lines in Sussex. Between 1959 and 1960 the original eighteen units had a centre carriage added, making them three-car units. These were reclassified as 3H (Class 205) and four more three-car units were built. Finally, another seven seven-car sets were built for the Salisbury–Reading service. This brought the total number in the class to thirty-three. The latter had larger guards van, and were called Berkshire units. Some units had a large 'V' painted at one end, which denoted to platform staff which end of the unit the guards van was.

The units proved to be a financial success. Each unit was covering around 120,000 miles every year with fuel consumption at around 0.4 miles per gallon. Only two refuelling points were needed – Fratton and Eastleigh. Between them, the units were covering around 40,000 miles every week. The new timetable and cleaner trains led to a 29 per cent increase in passengers in the first six months of service. One downside of the high mileages achieved was that their brake blocks needed replacing nearly every week. The engines could go 150,000 between intermediate overhauls and, when major overhauls were needed after 450,000 miles, a spare engine would be fitted, with the old engine being sent away to be renovated.

As lines in the area became electrified, many units found their way eastwards where they could be seen on the Oxted lines or working from Hastings to Rye.

Hastings DMUs

Hampshire was not the only area to benefit from a new diesel service. Six-car units were also being built for the Hastings line and these would be run in two six-car sets. These had corridor access through each six-car set. They were powered by a diesel engine in each end carriage. The four-cylinder diesel engines were coupled to a six-pole generator and a 13.2 kW auxiliary generator. The main generator supplied two four-pole nose-suspended traction motors. The carriages had to be built to the restricted loading gauge demanded by the limited clearance through the tunnels.

Initially the service was shared with steam until enough units could be built at Eastleigh, with a full diesel service being envisaged for June 1958. There were thirty-seven six-car sets in all, five of which included a buffet. The first-class passengers could also enjoy a new design of seat, wherein the squab could be pulled out from the back, giving a less upright seating position.

Accidents

On 15 April at 4:47 p.m. at Portsmouth & Southsea Station, a set of coaches were being propelled by a 0-4-4T back to Platform 2 to form the 5:45 p.m. to Cardiff. The driver of this train misinterpreted a hand gesture by a shunter as permission to start. His train hit the 4:45 p.m. Portsmouth to Cardiff train that had just left Platform 5. Although there were a set of catch points, these did not stop the propelling movement, and the leading coach struck the Cardiff service between the second and third carriages, ripping open the latter, before getting jammed between that and a high retaining wall. Four passengers were seriously injured. The breakdown crane failed on its way to the site but, even so, all lines were fully operational by 10:50 a.m. the following day.

Another accident occurred at Herne Hill at 9:03 a.m. on 30 June, when a steam hauled express from Victoria to Dover Marine with Battle of Britain 34088 at the front ploughed into the back of a Schools class 4-4-0 that was running light engine in front of it. Neither train was derailed, possibly because the driver of the Schools saw the express bearing down on him and he accelerated as fast as he could. Seven coaches out of the ten-coach express were slightly damaged, and nineteen of the 270 passengers on board suffered minor injuries or shock. Another train was summoned to transfer the passengers and this left at 11:47 a.m. to continue their journey to Dover, where the ferry was held up for them. The accident had blocked the Up and Down Fast, the Down Slow and the Branch line, but the stricken engines and carriages were removed by 1:35 p.m. and a full service resumed. The blame was put on the driver of the express for running through a distant at caution and a home at danger.

There was an accident at Staines Central at 12:24 p.m. on 9 August, when an eight-car electric train left the station against a red signal and collided almost head-on with a light engine on a crossing. The eight-car unit consisted of two four-car sets which were made up of the 12:07 p.m. from Windsor, and the 12:02 p.m. from Weybridge that had been connected at Staines for the onward journey to Waterloo. After making the connection, the porter signalled to the guard that he had connected the two units and the guard, who had just loaded a pram into his van, saw that everybody had boarded and waved his green flag. The foreman raised his arm and the driver, who was looking backwards after receiving the all clear from the station staff and guard, pulled away without checking to see if the home signal was clear, which it wasn't. The train had travelled just over 200 yards when it met a Class 700 0-6-0 on a crossover, turning it onto its side. The tender remained upright but was derailed. Luckily, only twelve passengers were slightly injured and the motorman received just cuts and bruises, although his cab was extensively damaged. The engine driver suffered a broken leg. Cranes arrived from Feltham and Nine Elms and a clear-up operation had started by 2 p.m. and normal services were resumed by 8:16 p.m. Some services had to be rerouted during this period and buses stood in for other services but, amazingly, out of the 143 trains that left Waterloo during the evening rush hours, 113 arrived at their destinations either on time or under five minutes late.

On Wednesday 4 December at Lewisham, the worst accident in the history of the Southern Region occurred. It happened at 6:20 p.m. in thick fog when 34066 *Spitfire* on the 4:56 p.m. from Cannon Street to Ramsgate via Folkestone ran through a red light and into the back of a stationary ten-car electric unit, which was the 5:18 p.m. Charing Cross to Hayes service. This was standing at Parks Bridge Junction colour light home signal. This was on a gradient, so the driver had applied the air brakes. This made the impact harder. The body of the eighth coach of the electric was destroyed when the underframe of the ninth coach smashed through it. On the Ramsgate train, the leading coach and the tender were forced together, sending them sideways and demolishing the middle column and two heavy girders supporting the bridge carrying the Nunhead to Lewisham line over the four main lines. The bridge collapsed onto the trains below. Both trains were running late due to the foggy conditions and were packed out with over 2,000 passengers in total on the two trains. Eighty-nine passengers and the guard of the electric lost their lives. 109 were injured badly enough to be detained in hospital and a further sixty-seven sustained minor injuries.

Many passengers were stranded in London with many services having to be cancelled. The following morning, main line services were diverted to Victoria. Breakdown cranes were called in from Nine Elms, Bricklayers Arms, Stewarts Lane and Ashford. The first six carriages and the last seven of the Ramsgate train had remained upright and were towed away. The collapsed bridge and the crushed carriages had to be cut up on the spot and this task was not completed until 4 p.m. on Monday. Track staff then got to work relaying and re-ballasting the track. Normal services were resumed on Thursday 12 December at 5 a.m.

The conclusions reached by the official report into the accident put the blame solely on the driver of the Ramsgate train. He had gone past signal A42 at New Cross at green and, as he could not see them, wrongly assumed that the next signals, L16 and L17, would also be green. They were in fact double amber and amber. He also could not see the next signal, L18, and did not react until his fireman told him it was on red. The fireman was exonerated of any blame because, although all three signals were on his side, he had no reason to presume that his driver could not see them and as such was busy stoking the fire for the long run up to Knockholt. As with other accidents we have mentioned, it was stated in the report that a system of Automatic Train Control giving an audible warning in the cab whenever a signal other than green was passed would have stopped the accidents from happening. At this time it was being planned for the Western Section of the region. It was also stated in the report that steam was being replaced by electric and diesel multiple units, and the visibility from these cabs was vastly improved.

New Locos

20 March 1957 proved to be a historic day for Brighton Works, as the last-ever new engine to be built there – Std Class 4 2-6-4T 80154 – was outshopped. This was the only one of the class to be given the new British Railways insignia.

Class 2MT 2-6-2Ts continued to be built at Derby, with some being allocated to Southern sheds, Ashford and Ramsgate being the main recipients.

Diesel shunters were also being delivered and allocated to Hither Green and Brighton. They were numbered from 11220 onwards. These were renumbered into the D20xx series when BR changed their numbering system. Hither Green was also receiving some new 08 class shunters.

904 new carriages were also produced for DMU use.

The first of British Railways designed four-car EPB units were introduced. These were to work throughout the network, with the last one being withdrawn in 1995.

4,300 new wagons were built at Ashford out of a total of 7,480 built countrywide.

End of Class

1957 saw the demise of Maunsell's N15X, 4-6-0s.

Facts and Figures

In 1957 there was another working deficit of £27 million. This figure did not take into account the £41 million of central charges and interest payments. Parliament had authorised the railways to borrow £250 million to help finance the 'Modernisation Plan', so this figure was about in line to what was expected; however, the staff were told that savings would have to be made by pruning little-used services and increasing productivity by employing fewer staff.

Freight traffic was beginning to drop, with over a million tons less being moved than in 1956. There were plans to build twenty-seven new marshalling yards and modernise another twenty-six. On the downside, 158 yards were due to close with another thirty-seven being partially closed. The 'Economic Commission for Europe' had stated that the utilisation of wagons, and their turn round on British Railways, was the worst in any Western European country.

The railways were still responsible for transporting over 82 million parcels every year.

It was agreed to spend £5 million on the electrification of the lines from Gillingham to Maidstone East, Sevenoaks, Sheerness, Margate, Folkestone and Dover.

Miscellanea

Cannon Street station had its platforms lengthened to accommodate ten-coach trains. Until then, the only London terminus on the Eastern Section that could handle ten-car trains was Charing Cross. Other stations were undergoing the same treatment so that longer trains could be handled. These included Bournemouth West where longer trains to the Midlands via the Somerset & Dorset were needed. In Surrey, new housing estates at Crawley and Merstham were leading to overcrowding on London bound trains, so platforms were lengthened at Coulsdon South, Redhill and Purley.

Part of Brighton Works, which was due to close, was to be leased to a British company building German designed Messerschmitt lightweight three-seater cars under licence. It was hoped that some of the railway staff would find employment there. An enthusiasts special visited the works, which was described by one visitor as 'forlorn'. An idea was put forward that the works should become part of the BTC museum.

Fuel rationing ended but it was becoming clear that the railways had started to lose much of the traffic they had gained from people and goods, which had been forced off the road by the shortages.

E1 4-4-0s were a 1920 Maunsell rebuild of a Wainwright design dating from 1905. 31506 was photographed on 25 May 1957. The bridge it is passing under was known as Welcome Bridge, between Gomshall and Dorking Town on the Guildford–Redhill line.

30582 was a 4-4-2T Class 0415 famous for working over the branch to Lyme Regis where this image was taken on 26 June 1956. It was designed by Adams as long ago as 1882. Only three survived in BR ownership and these only did so as they were the only locos that could negotiate the sharp bends on the Lyme Regis branch.

31177 was an H class 0-4-4 tank waiting to leave Westerham on 6 April 1957. It was a Wainwright design for the SECR in 1904. 31177 was introduced in March 1909 and withdrawn in October 1961.

Class E1/R 32135 heads Class N 31834 on a long freight trundling through Exeter Central.

AIX 32670 at St Leonards. It has been preserved and is working on the KESR, renumbered as No. 3 and named *Bodiam*.

Bournemouth West was the location of push pull fitted M7 30059. The loco lasted until February 1961 when it was withdrawn.

An ex-GWR engine on Southern metals, Class 4300 2-6-0 6318 is at Basingstoke with an express from Wolverhampton. (Courtesy Ben Brooksbank)

32349 was a 2-6-0 K class built for the LBSCR in 1913. There were seventeen of the class built and they were all withdrawn at the end of 1962.

Another O2 on the Isle of Wight was 24 *Calbourne*, photographed on Ryde's pierhead.

Class M7 0-4-4T 30025 on shed at Salisbury. It was withdrawn at the end of May 1964.

30270, photographed at Salisbury, was a class G6 introduced by Adams for the L&SWR in 1894. This example was withdrawn in February 1959.

Eastleigh was the scene of this image of H15 30488. It was introduced in 1914, giving good service for forty years before being withdrawn in May 1959.

30796 *Sir Dodinas Le Savage* was spotted at Eastleigh on 9 November 1957. (Courtesy Charlie Verrall)

Class D1 31509 was on shed at Faversham on 16 April 1957. (Courtesy Charlie Verrall)

Leaving Eastleigh on 5 November 1957 with a Down freight was BR Class 3MT 2-6-2T 82015. (Courtesy Charlie Verrall)

At the same time and place as the image of 31509 on p. 106, Class C 31714 could also have been seen. (Courtesy Charlie Verrall)

Chapter 9

1958

New Gatwick Station

The new Gatwick Airport Station opened on 28 May 1958, with the original Gatwick Airport Station – built in 1935 – closing the day before. It occupied the site of the old Gatwick Racecourse Station. It consisted of six platforms, joined to the main airport buildings by stairs or by lift. Every platform could handle twelve-coach trains, with some trains being split or joining there.

Accidents

At 12:58 p.m. on 4 March, an accident occurred at Gloucester Road Junction near Norwood Junction. A parcels train making its way from Brighton to London Bridge collided with a four-car electric unit that had just left West Croydon bound for Victoria. There had been some confusion in the cab as there was a diversion from the usual route, since that had been closed to allow for repair work to take place. The driver thought that the route was clear for him, but when his train took a different route against a red light, he applied the brakes. It was too late. The front of his 2-6-0 N class loco struck the third carriage of the four-car electric unit. Damage was slight and only five passengers were slightly injured. The line was cleared by 11:53 p.m., but until then some services had to be diverted and passengers wishing to travel between West Croydon and Norwood Junction had to use the existing trolley bus service or the special buses that were laid on.

Another accident happened in North Kent at Maze Hill at 10:25 a.m. on 4 July. The 9:41 a.m. four-car electric from Gravesend Central to Charing Cross ran past a red signal and collided with a ten-coach train of empty coaching stock, headed by a class C 0-6-0, which was crossing the Up Main to the Down Main. The force of the impact drove the empty coaches back 11 yards and the loco was lifted off the track and embedded itself into the leading carriage. Remarkably, of the forty-three injured, only five needed to be detained in hospital, and their injuries were not too serious. Following trains had to be diverted via Blackheath and Charlton, but the line was cleared by 7:54 p.m. The motorman was found to be at fault because, although he admitted seeing the distant signal at caution, he failed to respond to the home at danger. The guard was also criticised for not keeping a proper lookout.

A derailment occurred at Borough Market Junction when the tenth coach of a twelve-car train derailed on a broken point. The ninth coach slewed across the track and tilted. Six passengers were injured, but not seriously. The viaduct on which the accident happened had to be supported from underneath before the breakdown cranes could start lifting operations. The line into Cannon Street reopened at 4:35 p.m. and Charing Cross at 8:25 p.m.

A serious accident happened in the throat of Eastbourne Station and was yet another accident caused by a driver passing a home signal at red. It was 7:29 a.m. on 25 August when the overnight sleeper from Glasgow, which was entering Eastbourne, hit a twelve-car electric unit that was just leaving for Victoria. The force of the impact pushed the twelve-car 6-PUL/6-PAN formation back into the buffers. The Black 5 at the head of the sleeper and the leading carriage of the electric were thrown into the air, with both ending up on their sides. The closing speed of the two trains was around 25 mph. Four passengers and the motorman were killed. Twenty-two passengers were hospitalised but only five detained. The driver of the sleeper said it was raining heavily and his view of the home signal obscured, but other witnesses state that the rain had stopped and that he was entering the station too fast. Although he was not a regular driver on the route, he was fully trained to operate it, and the two overbridges on the approach to the station are very distinctive, so he had no excuse for either his speed or for not recognising the signal. He was found to be solely to blame.

A less serious accident happened at Tunbridge Wells on 22 December at 1:00 p.m. It involved two of the Hastings six-car diesel multiple units; 1017 and 1035. One of the units had arrived at Tunbridge Wells Central. A similar unit was supposed to couple up to it to form a twelve-car train to Charing Cross, but this unit approached too fast, causing damage to both cabs. The motorman of the second unit and two passengers were detained in hospital. A breakdown train arrived from Tonbridge, hauled by C class 31037. One of the cab sides of 1035 had been pushed out over the loading gauge and this had to be cut off with oxy-acetylene equipment before the unit could be towed away to Tunbridge Wells West, before then being taken away to Eastleigh for repair. These units were new and others in the class were still being built and delivered.

New Locos

The first of the new Bo-Bo electric locomotives was outshopped from Doncaster. Numbered E5000, it was delivered to Stewarts Lane (73A) on 24 December.

Six new 4-BEP/CEP units were being produced at Eastleigh every month ready for the Kent Coast electrification.

Loco Movements

Towards the end of the year, the last surviving Brighton Atlantic 32424 *Beachy Head* was often in charge of the weekday Brighton–Bournemouth service. It was also used on Christmas parcels trains to London. After Christmas, it was out of use at Brighton and would be withdrawn after working an enthusiasts' special in April '59.

The Brighton Works shunter 377S had to go into the works for repair and was replaced by 32646, which arrived from Fratton.

With the imminent electrification of lines in Kent, the King Arthurs employed there were having their six-wheeled tenders replaced by the eight-wheeled bogie type, ready for when they were allocated to the Western Section.

The Duke of Edinburgh visited Deal on 19 November and an immaculate Schools, *Brighton,* was in charge of a three-coach train that included the Pullman *Orion.* The loco was then used to pull a special train for the press to view the progress of the Kent Coast electrification.

On 2 December, the 9:00 a.m. Dover boat train hauled by 34088 *213 Squadron* slipped to a halt when climbing Grosvenor Bank out of Victoria and had to wait for assistance from a banking engine.

End of Classes

The last of Marsh's H2 4-4-2s were withdrawn from service.

Facts and Figures

BTC reported losses of £90.1 million, which included £42 million of interest and other central charges. This loss was higher than envisaged, due to a severe decline in heavy industrial production in the second half of the year. This had a knock-on effect on the railways, which showed a sharp downturn in the amount of coal and steel moved. The authorisation to borrow £250 million was increased to £400 million.

The staff were told not to be despondent about the financial situation as a speeding-up of the Modernisation Plan was sure to bring immediate improvements. This would have to be combined with further improved productivity and more unprofitable services being cut. Diesel multiple unit services were being welcomed by the public and whole areas would soon be free of any steam services. Staff were told that old ideas had to be scrapped and new ideas adopted to match the physical modernisation that was happening.

Nationally, 1,863 new passenger carriages were built, which included 286 carriages for EMUs and 1,070 for DMUs. Eighty-four of the 286 carriages for EMUs made up the first twenty-one units built for the Kent Coast electrification.

Only 36,284 new wagons were built compared to over 59,000 in 1957 and 61,000 in 1956. 121,000 wagons were withdrawn. The 1955 'Modernisation Plan' planned for a fleet of wagons numbering 750,000. Only wagons of larger carrying capacity were planned and the last 16-ton wagon had been completed, with all future wagons having a capacity of 20 tons.

The number of steam engines left in service dropped to 16,103 by the end of the year.

2,422 DMU vehicles were in use, with nearly half of them being under one year old. 317 more diesel shunters were introduced during the year.

Only seventy-five horses remained and these were all employed within yards and all deliveries were now done with motorised transport.

Miscellanea

Freight services were being challenged by an increase in 'C' licence holders, who had topped the 1 million mark. These were road vehicles that companies owned to transport their own goods. Many of these were vans that only operated locally but, increasingly, they were larger vehicles that transported goods that used to go by rail.

The British Railways Productivity Council had been set up in 1955 and, in 1958, had devised plans for Work Study techniques. Over 20,000 staff were then working on schemes that had been the result of these studies.

Class D1 31492 at an unknown location on 16 March 1958. This was a Maunsell rebuild of Wainwright's D Class of 1901. It was nearing the end of its life, being withdrawn in January 1960.

T9 30120 was in charge of the RCTS special 'The Sapper' when seen at Bookham on 4 October 1958. The tour had left Waterloo for a visit to the Longmoor Military Railway.

2-NOL 1820 enters Aldrington Halt on 1 February 1958. In 1934–6 they were converted from steam hauled stock and were all withdrawn by the end of 1959. (Courtesy Edwin Wilmshurst)

20001, introduced in 1941, was looking very smart when photographed at Eastleigh Works some years later. In later days it had a destination blind fitted between the cab windows.

Class D1 31727 enters Ashford with a train for Maidstone East on 8 March 1958.

A 4-COR passes Weybridge Station on 1 April 1958 on the 13:54 Waterloo–Portsmouth Harbour service. (Courtesy Ben Brooksbank)

34085 *501 Squadron* heads a boat train through Tonbridge on 4 May 1958.

Chapter 10

1959

Kent Coast Electrification

To accommodate the twelve-car electric trains that were being planned for the London–Faversham electrification scheme, Dover Marine had to undergo extensive alterations. The two island platforms had to be extended by 114 feet. This necessitated the re-laying of the tracks in the station throat. The covered walkway to the train ferry dock was also replaced with a footbridge from the street entrance to link up with the existing walkway. Signals also had to be resited. Power operated pointwork was installed and steam pipes for carriage heating were laid to all four platforms. This work required the closing of the station for a week at the end of February; some of the cross-Channel ferries had to be diverted to Folkestone during that time.

Stage 1 of the electrification of Kent lines was completed in June. Lines that were electrified were Faversham via Dover Priory to Dover Marine, and the Dover Triangle. More than 150 route miles were involved and this entailed rebuilding five stations and installing nine sub-stations. Extensive earthworks were involved between Folkestone Central and Cheriton, where the line was quadrupled. The colour light signals already operating as far as Hither Green were extended to Ramsgate, meaning a two-and-a-half minute headway could be maintained from the Capital to Swanley, with three minutes between there and the coast. This meant that eight new power signal boxes had to be opened. These were at Shepherds Lane, Brixton, Beckenham Junction, Shortlands, Chiselhurst Junction, Rochester, Rainham, Sittingbourne and Faversham. Semaphores were kept from there to Dover. These improvements were expected to accelerate services to the port.

Large sections of track were also re-laid with the least disruption to services as possible. One such section was between Shortlands Junction through Shortlands, Bromley South and Bickley Stations to Bickley Junction. The section originally comprised two Up lines running parallel with two Down lines, with sharp bends at either end involving speed restrictions of 20 mph at Shortlands and 30 mph at Bickley. This layout also meant that slow trains had to cross fast lines causing delays. The stretch was redesigned so that the Up and Down slow lines were adjacent to each other, as were the fast lines. Crossovers were laid to allow change of route or line switch between fast and slow lines. The work involved big earthworks, the reconstruction of sixteen bridge spans, and the removal of ten bridges. The work was done over every weekend from October 1958 until May 1959. The junctions were made to measure at New Cross Gate at the District Engineers depot. These junctions were then cut into lengths that could fit onto 'Bo-Rail' wagons and transported to the site where they were laid in place. Up to twelve engineers' trains would leave New Cross Gate on a Saturday night, which caused problems in finding enough locos and crews, as the normal service was still running. Most of the work was done between midnight on Saturdays and 10 a.m. on Sundays, although a few track possessions lasted twenty-four or even thirty hours. On the weekend of 6/7 September 1958, three lines had to be slewed into new positions over half a mile in length, with a maximum skew of 4 feet on the slow line and to lesser extents on two fast lines. A double junction had to be removed and replaced with a faster running one. Two 60-foot bridges had to be skewed by 1 foot 6 inches to accommodate the new alignment. The Up slow line was reopened at 9 a.m. on Sunday morning and the Down slow line one hour later, while the two fast tracks were still being worked on. These final two tracks were opened at 4 a.m. on Monday morning.

Following the completion of the first phase of electrification, Gillingham (73D), Faversham (73E) and Ramsgate (73G) lost their allocations of steam locomotives. Gillingham and Ramsgate became sub-depots while Faversham was converted to a diesel depot.

The first electric train to run all the way from Victoria Ramsgate was the 8:00 a.m. on 2 June. The nine coaches were hauled by electric locomotive E5004. A second train that afternoon was hauled by sister loco E5003. The following day, a twelve-car electric train left Cannon Street for Ramsgate, made up of 7138/41/2. On 9 June an inaugural run of the new electric units was run for the benefit of the Minister of Transport and the press, which visited Dover and Margate. Units 7003/4/5 were used on various parts of the trip. The first public trip was the Night Ferry on 8 June, behind E5003.

From 15 June all services were in the hands of the new electrics and steam services ended, although the new service got off to an inauspicious start when 7111 failed at Dover early in the morning and subsequent trains had to be cancelled.

Fifty-three new four-car electric units, 4-CEP (Corridor Electro-Pneumatic Brake), were introduced to operate the express services. Ten of these units were fitted with buffet facilities, with the buffet coaches allowing seating for seventeen passengers (4-BEP Buffet Electro-Pneumatic Brake).

For intermediate services there were another sixty-two two-car units.

A second stage of electrification was planned, comprising the route from Sevenoaks to Tonbridge and Ashford, then to Ramsgate via Canterbury West and Dover, Folkestone, Deal and Ramsgate.

Baggage vans were attached to the rear of the trains. These would be detached by shunters and taken to the quayside for loading on to ferries. Ten battery-driven vans were to be built to negate the need for a shunter. These were classified as MLV and numbered 68001–10. They had enough power in their batteries to operate for up to twenty minutes. They had a full-width cab at either end to allow them to be at the front or rear of trains. They were needed as it was impracticable to lay conductor rails onto tracks sunk into the quayside.

New Class 71 Electric Locos

New electric locomotives in the E5XXX series were being delivered to Stewarts Lane. They were designed to handle heavy freight services on the South Eastern section of the region, with 900 tons being within their capabilities. On 9 June, however, they were all temporarily withdrawn because E5001 had suffered a brake problem while on a training run. A brake block had fallen off while running at speed, damaging the leading coaches of its train. Examination revealed that the brake shoe holders had been incorrectly made and safety straps were missing.

By September, nine had been delivered and had been used on the heavy Night Ferry service and on the Newhaven boat train, which they shared with the earlier Southern electric locomotives 20001–3. They were also used to haul the prestigious Golden Arrow. The original order had been for thirteen but this was increased to twenty-four. Their curved sides conformed to that of modern rolling stock. They had a top speed of 90 mph and were powered by third rail, so could not work on un-electrified lines. However, they were also fitted with pantographs, so they could work off overhead lines where third rail was considered too dangerous; for example, Hither Green yard and Snowdown Colliery. The overhead collection apparatus was of a simple tram type pole, as there were no places where high-speed collection was needed. As Hither Green and other places lost their overhead systems, the pantographs were removed. They were hindered by not having separate diesel engines, as they could not be used on engineer's trains when the power was cut, or at night when engineers were working on the line and it necessitated the power being cut.

Bluebell Railway

On 15 March, the Lewes & East Grinstead Railway Preservation Society was formed with a view to reopening the line from East Grinstead to Culver Junction near Lewes, which had recently been closed by BR. The initial aim was to run a DMU service over the whole line. When it became obvious there was no local appetite for the venture, the group's aim was changed to operating a preservation railway between Horsted Keynes and Sheffield Park, using vintage steam engines and stock. They also changed their name to the Bluebell Railway Preservation Society, and the first railway preservation society in the world was formed.

Accidents

On 18 February between Slade Green and Dartford, one electric train ran into the back of another in thick fog. The 9:40 a.m. Charing Cross to Gillingham had been halted at a red signal when the 9:25 a.m. Charing Cross to Dartford ran into the back of it. Seventeen passengers were taken to hospital but only one was detained. The accident was blamed on the signalmen of Crayford Spur A and Slade Green boxes who, owing to a misunderstanding, had overridden the safety systems and allowed the latter train into the occupied section.

Two other minor accidents occurred. On 31 October, EMU 7111 became derailed at Dover, hitting the brickwork of a tunnel. At Faversham on 10 November, D5000 was hauling a coal train from Snowdown Colliery when it ran away out of control and into a sand drag, demolishing a buffer before hitting the main line track and buckling it.

New Locos

Seven diesels, D5000–D5006, had been delivered to Hither Green from Derby. These were on loan until the new Class 33 diesels were delivered. The first of these, D6500, arrived at Hither Green on 17 December.

Also delivered new were some diesel shunters – D3665–D3669 built at Darlington and D2882/3 built at Doncaster.

Loco Movements

The light Pacifics were being rebuilt at Eastleigh. Five of these – 34039, 34045, 34046, 34047 and 34048 – had been shedded at Brighton, but after being rebuilt they were transferred to Nine Elms, and Brighton was allocated another five unrebuilt engines. The last ten Merchant Navies were undergoing the same treatment at Eastleigh.

A number of ex-GWR locos were loaned to the Southern. These included 2-6-0 7303 to Bath (Radstock) while 11 0-6-0PTs went to Nine Elms for ECS duties, or Folkestone for banking duties.

As part of the Transport Commission's 'Transport Treasures Exhibition', A1X 82 *Boxhill*, and Adams ex-LSWR, class T3 4-4-0 563 were displayed at Salisbury during February. They both travelled north during April and were on show at York in May and Carlisle during July. Class D 4-4-0 31737 joined them during June. They were then temporarily stored at Tweedmouth (52D), before all three made their way south again via Newcastle, York and Didcot.

Bulleid's diesel mechanical shunter 11001 was withdrawn in August after being in store at Ashford for some time.

Horsham shed closed on 18 July and its allocation of M7s 30047/8/9/50/1 went to Brighton and Qs 30544/56/7, E4s 32463/9/70 and C2Xs 32522/6/41 went to Three Bridges. However one Q, one E4 and three Hs would continue to be stabled there overnight.

All the engines that had been allocated to the Eastern Section were reallocated to Nine Elms. This meant that their allocation increased by 106 new locos almost overnight, although in reality it took a while for them all to arrive. One of the biggest changes was that the Schools class were to be seen on Southampton boat trains and semi-fasts to Basingstoke out of Waterloo. Other members of the class were used on the Brighton–Bournemouth service.

From June, the D5xxx were used on the Margate to Birkenhead service with double heading being required on Saturdays when loads were heavier.

End of Classes

A number of classes disappeared from the region during the year, including Adams's 0395 0-6-0, Drummond's S14, 0-4-0Ts and Billinton's E3, 0-6-2Ts.

Facts and Figures

The number of steam locos had been reduced to 14,452 by the end of the decade. The introduction of the Class 71s for the Southern had helped increase the nation's number of electric locos to eighty-five. There were also 1,800 diesels in service by the end of the decade.

There were still roughly the same number of passenger coaches as at the start of the decade, the figure of which was just over 40,000. Freight wagons, however, had halved from 1,197,561 to 960,353. There had been a switch to containers though with an increase from 19,966 in 1948 to just over 50,000 in 1959.

The working losses in 1959 amounted to over £42 million, which at least was £6 million less than the previous years.

Passenger journeys had held up well over the decade with an increase of 5 million to 240 million, whereas freight had dropped from 124 million to 107 million tons.

Miscellanea

The 'B4's were banned from working over electrified lines when one had a mishap at Dover docks with the protective boarding for a conductor rail.

The new Hampshire DMUs were suffering from hot axle boxes during hot weather.

The Carriage & Wagon Works at Eastleigh had been experimenting with making doors from polyester resin reinforced fibre glass. Problems had been encountered in the past with water ingress through the opening windows forming rust on the metal sheets that had been used to cover the wooden framework. The new doors were made of two laminates jointed during the process with a green pigment added to the resin. Two patterns were being produced – one suitable for Southern stock and the other for BR MK1 standard doors. Four hundred were already in service by May. They were found to be lighter and more durable than the doors they replaced.

A pair of L class 4-4-0 locos, 31760 and 31768, operated a special to the Kent & East Sussex Railway on 18 October '59. This pair pulled the train to Robertsbridge, from where a pair of A1Xs, 32670 and DS680, topped and tailed the train for a return trip to Tenterden.

2-NOL 1814 enters Horsted Keynes on a train from Seaford. (Courtesy: Edwin Wilmshurst)

The Brighton Belle makes its way south through the Sussex countryside in 1959. (Courtesy: Edwin Wilmshurst)

34018 *Axminster* was on Nine Elms shed when photographed here. It had been modified in October 1958 and was one of the last to survive, being withdrawn in 1967.

A brace of L class locos, 31760 and 31768, operated a special to the KESR on 18 October 1959.

The driver climbs aboard his steed, 34052 *Lord Dowding*, at Nine Elms before he heads off to Waterloo to pick up his train for another trip westwards.

Merchant Navy class 35009 *Shaw Savill* heads out of Salisbury.

A 6-PUL unit, 3008, waits to leave Eastbourne on a semi-fast service to Victoria.

Two views of Schools class 4-4-0 30915 *Brighton*, in the station of the same name. Above, the driver takes a well-earned breather after bringing his train safely to the buffers while, below, the same train from the other direction. The headcode would indicate that the train had arrived from Salisbury and travelled via Eastleigh. (Both courtesy Ian D. Nolan)

H Class 31276 at Hove Station on its way to Horsham in the late 1950s. (Courtesy Ian D. Nolan)

BR Std 4MT 4-6-0 75075 at Hove Station. (Courtesy Ian D. Nolan)

Summary

The 1950s had been a fairly successful for the railways. They had recovered from the very poor state they were left in after the war and towards the end of the decade some of the investments made in the system were beginning to be seen.

On the Southern, the largest investment had been in the extension of the Kent electrification scheme, but, on the downside, savings were being made by some rural stations and branch lines being closed, with still more under threat of closure.

Nationally, the stock of steam locomotives fell from 19,598 to 14,452, whereas electric locomotives rose from seventeen to eighty-five, and diesels from 128 to 1,800. Coaching stock remained fairly stable – only falling from 42,218 to 40,537. Freight vehicle numbers fell from 1,122,215 to 960,353, indicating the increased threat coming from road haulage. Tonnage of freight moved fell from 281 million to 234 million over the decade.

Nearly 1,000 route miles of track were closed, but passenger journeys increased from 982 million to 1.045 billion. There was a slight increase in passenger train mileage run – from 235 million to 240 million – with freight trains running 107 million miles in 1959 compared to 124 million in 1950.

From the passengers' point of view, most of the changes were welcome. Smelly, dirty steam engines were beginning to give way to cleaner, smarter diesel multiple units.

From the steam enthusiast's point of view, the changes were not so good. Many of the classes of locos that dated back to pre-grouping days were getting rarer or had already disappeared and were replaced by newer Standard types or even diesels.

These changes were just a foretaste of things to come during the 1960s!